EXPLORER

Baku
MINI VISITORS' GUIDE

www.liveworkexplore.com

Baku Mini **Visitors'** Guide
ISBN – 978-9948-441-90-8

Copyright © Explorer Group Ltd 2011
All rights reserved.

All maps © Explorer Group Ltd 2011

Front cover photograph: Maiden's Tower – Pete Maloney

Contributing photographer – Mamed Rahimov

Printed and bound by
Emirates Printing Press, Dubai, UAE

Explorer Publishing & Distribution
PO Box 34275, Dubai, United Arab Emirates
Phone +971 (0)4 340 8805   Fax +971 (0)4 340 8806
info@explorerpublishing.com
www.explorerpublishing.com

While every effort and care has been made to ensure the accuracy of the information contained in this publication, the publisher cannot accept responsibility for any errors or omissions it may contain.

No part of this publication may be reproduced, stored in a retrieval system, or transmitted, in any form or by any means, electronic, mechanical, photocopying, recording or otherwise, without the prior permission in writing of the publisher.

Welcome...

Welcome to the *Baku Mini Visitors' Guide*. This mini marvel has been passionately prepared by the same team that brought you the *Azerbaijan Explorer, Live Work Explore*. Written entirely by residents, and perfect for visitors, you'll find all you need to make the most out of your time in this interesting metropolis – whether it is the top restaurants, the most stylish shops or the best cultural spots.

Baku is a dynamic city with an ever-changing skyline, and *Explorer* brings you the insider knowledge. With more and more luxury openings on the horizon we have included the very best of this extraordinary city today, as well as what to look out for in the future. And we have not forgotten the past – from the most revealing historical sites to the most fascinating places to wander, we help you to find your way around and to the heart of the city.

The **Pull-Out Map** at the back of the book will help with navigation, while **Essentials** (p.2) tells you all you need to ensure a memorable trip. Turn to **Shopping** (p.130) for the best souvenir spots, **Going Out** (p.154) for eating and entertainments, **Spas & Sports** (p.114) for all sorts of activities and **Exploring** (p.66) for, well, happy exploring!

The Explorer Team

Contents

Essentials — 2
- Welcome To Baku — 4
- Culture & Heritage — 6
- Modern Baku — 16
- Baku Checklist — 18
- Best Of Baku — 28
- Visiting Baku — 30
- Local Knowledge — 38
- Media & Further Reading — 48
- Public Holidays & Annual Events — 50
- Getting Around — 52
- Places to Stay — 58
- Beach Hotels — 67

Exploring — 66
- Explore Baku — 68
- At a Glance — 72
- The Boulevard — 72
- Old City (Icheri Sheher) — 74
- Downtown Baku — 80
- Around The City — 82
- Art Galleries — 84
- Museums — 88
- Theatres & Entertainment Venues — 92
- Parks, Beaches & Attractions — 96
- Tours & Sightseeing — 102
- Further Out — 104

Spas & Sports — 114
- Active Baku — 116
- Spas & Fitness — 118
- Sports & Activities — 122
- Spectator Sports — 126

Shopping — 130
- Buying In Baku — 132
- Where To Go For… — 136
- Areas To Shop — 146
- Markets & Bazaars — 148
- Shopping Malls & Department Stores — 152

Going Out — 154
- Dine, Drink, Dance — 156
- Entertainment — 162
- Restaurants & Cafes — 174
- Bars & Clubs — 192

Index — 204

www.liveworkexplore.com

Essentials

Welcome To Baku	4
Culture & Heritage	6
Modern Baku	16
Baku Checklist	18
Best Of Baku	28
Visiting Baku	30
Local Knowledge	38
Media & Further Reading	48
Public Holidays & Annual Events	50
Getting Around	52
Places To Stay	58
Beach Hotels	67

Essentials

Welcome To Baku

Welcome to Baku, capital of the Caucasus and a 21st century boomtown that's an intriguing mix of east and west.

Baku's transformation from neglected Soviet outpost to an internationally important city has been a rapid one. The capital of Azerbaijan, one of the three nations that make up the Transcaucasus region, has announced itself onto the world stage in fairly dramatic fashion over the last decade. A hydrocarbon-fuelled economic explosion has seen money pouring into Baku, bringing with it a raft of upmarket shops, five-star hotels and glitzy bars, and reinforcing a thriving cultural and arts scene.

It is a constantly changing city. The skyline is unrecognisable, even from two years ago. City planners are working hard to make Baku a desirable destination both for tourists and international workers. Wide, multi-lane highways have replaced the bumpy single-carriage roads; bridges and parks have been bedecked in marble (not least the overhauled Boulevard centrepiece, which runs along the Caspian shore); and utilitarian apartment blocks have been reclad in soft yellow stone and given ornate finishes. All of this is designed to match modern Baku, with its array of funky high-rise buildings and designer boutiques.

And as more expats and foreign visitors are drawn to town by these new developments, the older, more traditional attractions, such as the Old City and mugham music, have benefited too from increased attention, and become worthy highlights in their own right. The traditional beauty and appeal of Baku is more apparent now than ever before and, to complement it, there is a real buzz to the place.

The bustling, cosmopolitan nature of this thriving city is in marked contrast to the rest of Azerbaijan. From the snow-covered northern Caucasus mountains to the lush green sub-tropical south, the expansive central plains to the dusty desert-industrial Absheron Peninsula upon which Baku sits, there is an intriguing patchwork of people and places to be explored by the intrepid traveller keen to see beyond the city limits.

This book sets out to bring you all the information needed to get the most out of a visit to this up and coming city. This chapter, Essentials, provides a flavour of the place by delving into the country's history, examining the way it functions today, and telling you what you need to know to get around. It also highlights some of the must-do activities and sights, as well as the best places to stay. The Exploring chapter (p.66) looks in more detail at what to see in Baku and beyond, covering the city's museums, galleries and heritage sites. Spas & Sports (p.114) gives ideas on where to go for pampering, or some rather more exerting sporting activities should you prefer. Shopping (p.130) gives you the need-to-know information on all things retail, and finally Going Out (p.154) guides you through the major dining, drinking and entertainment hotspots of this increasingly popular Caspian playground.

Culture & Heritage

Baku's development into a major capital is set against a backdrop of complex cultural history and major regional power shifts.

Early Azerbaijan & The Arrival Of Islam

While Azerbaijan as an independent state, with Baku as its capital, is a relatively recent entity, the history of the area that the modern country now encompasses stretches back several millennia, and incorporates a complex mix of people, religions and influencing forces.

Zoroastrianism was one of the early religions to spread through the region, from around the 6th century BC, when it was part of the Persian Empire, and fire temples were a key part of the local form of worship. Their legacy can be seen today close to Baku at Ateshgah (see p.105).

The Caucasian Albanian influence then led to a period of Christianity in the area, which remained from around the third century AD to the eighth century – when Islam arrived. The Arab Caliphate introduced the new religion when it swept into the region.

For the next thousand or so years different empires came and went, and a number of groups sprung up in what is now Azerbaijan. Oguz and Seljuk Turks arrived and settled, shaping the language and ethnicity of the region, and it

Glimpses of Baku's rich cultural heritage

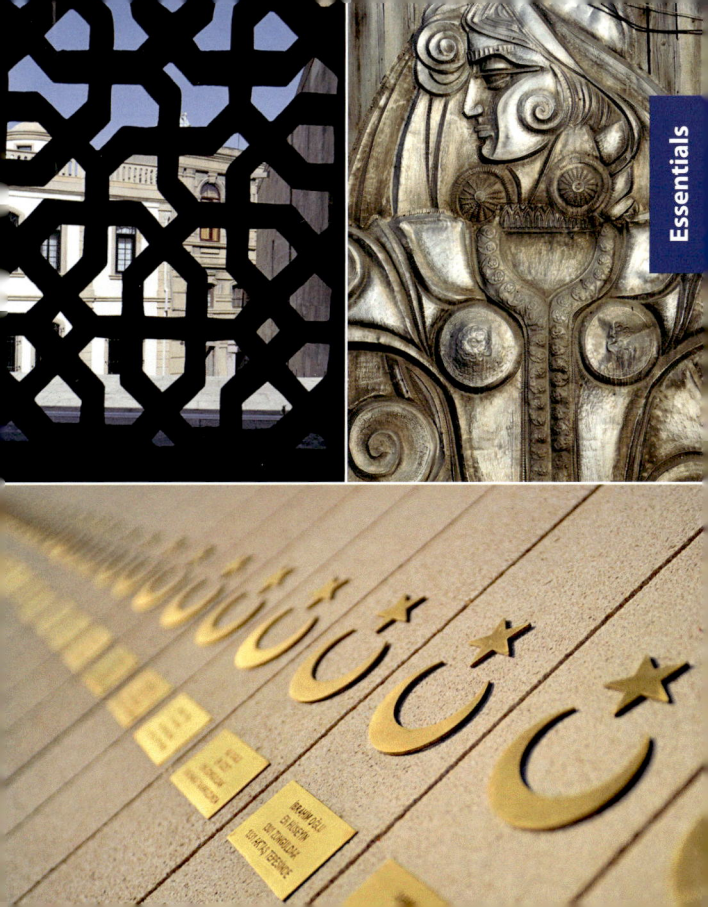
Essentials

was at the tail end of this period, in the 12th century, that a golden age of classic Azerbaijani culture occurred. With its capital as Shamakhi, the state that was now known as Shirvan flourished, becoming an influential regional presence.

Baku's Origins

When an earthquake ravaged Shamakhi, the capital was shifted to the small coastal trading town of Baku, which had a more favourable defensive position. The result was the development of the early stages of what is now known as Baku's Old City, including Maiden's Tower (p.78).

In the 13th century Asia's most notorious uninvited guests, the marauding Mongols, arrived, demolished cities and brought the region to its knees. Things picked up again by the 15th century, the era when monuments such as the Shirvanshah Palace (p.75) were constructed. After a number of conflicts and regional tussles, the Shirvans linked up with the Safavids to the south (in modern-day Iran) to become the core of the resurgent Persian Empire for the next few centuries, with the centre of power shifting south to Tabriz.

Border Battles

By the 18th century, a new three-way power tussle between the region's dominant empires – the Persians, the Ottomans and the Russians – had a major bearing on Azerbaijan's destiny. Battles were fought over the territory, culminating in the carving up of the Caucasus by the victorious Russians in the form of the Turkmenchay Treaty in 1828, which established today's basic territorial borders and saw

Azerbaijan come under Russian influence. It was later on during the 19th century that Baku's big transformation took place – namely the new commoditisation of oil and the exploitation of the bountiful reserves of it on the Absheron Peninsula. This was the catalyst for the capital's shift from small town to booming city at the turn of 20th century, with oil money funding construction, expansion and prosperity for many.

Soviet Rule

World War One and the collapse of the Russian Empire in 1917 led to another change in direction for Azerbaijan – a short-lived period of independence, brought to a sudden end by the arrival of the Soviets. The Red Army arrived in 1920 and by 1922 had created the Transcaucasian Soviet Socialist Republic, which grouped Azerbaijan together with Armenia and Georgia. By 1936 Azerbaijan was fully integrated as a republic of the Soviet Union. Integration into the USSR dampened the spiralling growth and accumulation of wealth in Baku, and a period of neglect as Soviet focus switched to other regions of the union left the city stagnating for several decades.

Modern Times

After the Soviet Union crumbled (but sadly not before Soviet forces massacred 200 protesters in Baku), Azerbaijan became independent once more in 1991, opening the way for the capital to take economic advantage of its most prized resource again. Foreign oil companies were invited back to town, and brought with them wealthy expats. In 2005, the Baku-Tbilisi-Ceyhan pipeline came into operation, cementing Baku's position as a major 21st century exporter. While much of the money has ended up directly benefiting only a small section of society, some of it has been used to polish up a shabby city, and the oil industry has had the knock-on effect of attracting other businesses, including construction firms and major hotel chains. Quite a transformation for a previously unfashionable Soviet outpost.

The Aliyev Family

The country's president is Ilham Aliyev – and if you spend just a short amount of time in Baku you'll quickly notice that the Aliyev family is something of a modern-day political dynasty in Azerbaijan. When Ilham took over leadership of the YAP party and the country in 2003 he succeeded his father Heydar, who had been president since 1993. Memorials to Heydar Aliyev can be found in Baku and cities around the country in many forms, from statues and parks to street names and buildings.

Culture

Azerbaijan's position in the Caucasus, physically and metaphorically a bridge between two continents, has been instrumental in shaping its culture over the centuries, with elements of both east and west, and Europe and Asia, evident in its people and its histories. It's a Muslim country, but a liberal one unlike its southern and eastern neighbours. It's a former Soviet country, with all the hallmarks and legacies that brings, but it has worked hard to regain its own identity and heritage since the break-up of the union two decades ago. Azeri has been officially reinstated as the main language, with street names and signs in Baku changed back from their old Cyrillic scripts. Other Soviet legacies, such as corruption, are proving a little harder to shake off. That's not to say that Russian influence is completely forgotten here; there are many Russian residents, particularly in Baku, and of course a high number of families have both Russian and Azeri blood intertwined. And, for the last century, since the start of the oil boom years, there's been a constant influx of international expats to Baku, bringing with them influences from their own countries.

There is a rich vein of purer Azeri heritage and culture that is woven into the fabric of the modern nation too: Baku's Old City is a living piece of architectural history; folk traditions live on through mugham music; and crafts such as carpet weaving are still important today. And throughout the country, both within the capital and without, the concept of family is particularly valued.

Baku itself is a liberal, tolerant city, more so than some of the country's regions. Unlike other more hardline Islamic countries, you won't see religion-influenced dress restrictions in the capital, and alcohol is openly served (and drunk). The politics of the country are similarly secular too. The arts also thrive in Baku, particularly music; jazz has a rich recent heritage, and is played in venues around town (see p.162), and large opera, ballet and theatre productions are frequently staged as well.

Ethnically speaking, the majority of the population is Azeri (see People & Economy, p.16), while ethnic minority groups with strong cultural identities include the Lezgins in the north (p.106) and Talysh in the south.

Food & Drink

Many international cuisines can be found in restaurants around Baku, catering for well-off locals and the cosmopolitan expat population. The quality can vary, and prices in the higher-end restaurants can be expensive, but it's there if you want it. Some cheaper local options are worth seeking out and the mainstream fastfood outlets also have a presence in the capital. See the Going Out chapter, p.154, for a detailed list of the options.

Traditional Azeri cuisine is very much influenced by the country's geographical position. It makes excellent use of the bountiful home-grown vegetables and fruits that are produced here, as well as herbs and spices. It also shares its culinary traditions with neighbouring countries.

Mugham

Mugham is Azerbaijan's celebrated traditional music form and, in 2003, was included in UNESCO's Intangible Cultural Heriage list. It's a fairly complex combination of classical, folk and free-form styles, and sounds very atmospheric – particularly when listened to live in an authentic setting, such as Karavan Saray (p.184) or the Mugham Club (p.186) in the Old City.

Alfresco evening dining

Popular dishes include *plov* or *pilau*, a rice dish that can be served with lamb, fish, or even dried fruit to create a sweet variation; kebabs; thick, stocky soups; and a variety of fish dishes, including *lavangi*, in which the fish is stuffed with minced walnut and onion.

Piles of vegetables and herbs, typically including cucumbers and tomatoes, are served at beginning of traditional Azeri dinners. A yoghurt and herb-based soup, known as *dovgha*, is often taken after the main course as a digestive aid, and tea – an integral part of local daily life (see Going Out, p.154) – is usually poured before dessert, which features sweet pastries and fruits.

Essentials

Despite being a Muslim country, alcohol is freely available, and there is a good range of regional wine, both Azeri and Georgian, to explore. Vodka is a notable legacy from the Soviet era. Pork is also available on most menus.

Religion

Islam is the dominant religion in Azerbaijan, with more than 90% of the population Muslim (mainly Shia). While religion is certainly important in the country, it is practised very moderately in this secular society, and the overriding attitude is one of tolerance. Under Soviet rule, religion was not looked upon particularly fondly, which has undoubtedly influenced the more liberal attitudes compared with regional neighbours such as Iran. Islamic culture and heritage can be found in some of the architecture around Baku, particularly in the domed roofs in the Old Town, but things like attitudes to women covering up and the consumption of alcohol are not strict, certainly in the capital (although in some regions, particularly Absheron, Islam is practised more conservatively). Fasting during Ramadan is followed by many, but not in the strict way it is in other countries, and life generally runs as normal during this period.

Other faiths are free to practise in Azerbaijan too; religious freedom is part of the Azerbaijani constitution. Sunni Muslim, Christian (including Catholics and Russian and Georgian Orthodox) and Jewish communities can all be found here, and some Muslims even follow a strand of Islam that incorporates some of the country's ancient animist traditions, which relates back to the region's Zoroastrian heritage.

National Dress

There's no modern-day national dress as such in Azerbaijan. In Baku, dress is fairly casual, and is not influenced by religion. Generally, women don't 'cover up', while trousers and shirts are the attire of habit for most men.

In fact, appearances suggest that men have more peer pressure to dress moderately than women – males wearing shorts are generally frowned upon, while younger females in Baku have a reputation for wearing more flashy clothing. Out in the regions, the attitude is again more conservative, which is something to bear in mind if you go exploring.

There is, however, a more traditional set of national costumes that is still proudly replicated today. Historically, materials varied according to social position. For women, two outer garments were worn, usually a blouse, shirt or waist-length tunic/jacket (*arkhaliq*, *ust koynek* or *chapkan*), combined with a skirt, and a large belt (*kamar*). Colourful headgear in the form of a shawl or embroidered cap was also worn.

Men's clothing consisted of wide pantaloons and a woollen coat or coat or jacket (*arkhaliq*) for the average citizen, and trousers, snugly fitted jacket (*chukha*) and a fleece coat (*kurk*) in winter for the upper echelons of society. A fluffy woollen upright hat (*papaq*), or sometimes a skull cap (*arakhchin*), was the essential accessory.

Beyond being featured on postcards, you might get the chance to actually see examples of traditional dress on major public holidays (p.51) and at some of Baku's main heritage attractions, such as Maiden's Tower (p.78).

Modern Baku

The export of hydrocarbons has been the main generating income for Baku, spurring breakneck development.

In stark contrast to the Soviet years, independent Azerbaijan has embraced the potential for growth that its huge amounts of hydrocarbon resources offer. The government has encouraged investment from the big international oil companies, and the new BTC (Baku-Tbilisi-Ceyhan) pipeline has turned Azerbaijan into a major exporter.

Baku has certainly been treated to something of a celebratory facelift, and you'll see evidence of this across the capital. Dilapidated old Soviet buildings have been restored to their grander days along the main thoroughfares; construction has mushroomed at sites all over town, with a five-star hotel rush giving that industry a timely boost; and designer boutiques on Neftchilar Prospect, and a brand new shopping mall, Park Bulvar, seek to get those who have prospered to swiftly depart with their newly acquired cash. Despite the rocky global economy, the demand for oil continues and so does modern Baku's potential for growth.

People & Economy

The population of Azerbaijan is estimated to be around nine million (including the half million or so people who live in Nakhchivan Autonomous Republic), according to official government sources, which makes the country the most populous of the Caucasus nations. Azerbaijan's urban-rural split is approximately 50:50, and more than two million people live in Baku, which is by far the country's largest city. Ganja, Azerbaijan's second-largest urban centre, has a population of just over 300,000.

The country's post-Soviet economic fortunes, led by Baku, have been driven by the hydrocarbons industry, and cemented by the opening of two major pipelines in the early 2000s (Baku-Tbilisi-Ceyhan and Baku-Tbilisi-Erzrum) that allowed Caspian oil and gas to be safely transported to all the major western markets. More than 60% of the economy falls directly into that industry's sector, but as with any economy heavily reliant on the export of hydrocarbons, there is a fairly pressing need to diversify. Tourism is certainly one sector that the authorities are attempting to exploit, and while infrastructure and income are currently still in their early infancy, the Ministry of Culture and Tourism is spearheading a campaign to vastly improve both the country's tourism potential and promotion.

A number of international hotel chains are currently developing a presence in Baku (Hilton, JW Marriott and Four Seasons are all due to open soon, while the Hyatt is already operational). Accessibility to some areas of interest in the rest of the country remains challenging (and often prohibitively expensive if you need to use the services of a tour company), but with a landscape of breathtaking diversity and a hospitable population, there is certainly huge potential to develop the sector with some serious investment over the next decade.

Essentials

Baku Checklist

01 Explore The Old City

There's no better way to get a feel for Baku's ancient heritage than meandering through the Old City. Catch tantalising glimpses of local daily life in the courtyards and narrow passages of this walled piece of living history, and get up close to the impressive medieval architecture of Shirvanshah's Palace. p.75.

Essentials

Baku Checklist

02 Take In The Views

The natural amphitheatre of Baku, spilling down towards the Caspian Sea, is best viewed from on high, and there are two excellent vantage points. Climb the narrow spiral stairs to the top of the iconic Maiden's Tower (p.78), or take a ride on the funicular railway (p.55) up to Martyrs' Alley to look back across the bay.

Essentials

Baku Checklist

03 Embrace The Music Scene
Azeris are proud of their musical heritage, so expect to see plenty of folk bands performing around town. They also dig their jazz music which is showcased at the annual International Jazz Festival (p.163). In 2011, Azerbaijan made its mark on the modern music scene, winning the hugely popular Eurovision Song Contest.

04 Venture Into Absheron

The spit of land jutting into the Caspian, on which Baku sits, has a number of sites worth visiting, including the Ateshgah Fire Temple, Gobustan Mud Volcanoes, and a number of beach resorts (p.64), all within an hour of Baku. And if you're adventurous, there's a whole beautiful, under-explored country to explore.

05 A Night At The Opera

Although getting into theatre and literature in Azerbaijan is pretty difficult if you don't speak Azeri, if there's one art form where not speaking the language won't inhibit your enjoyment, it has to be opera – and Baku stages some excellent productions at the Opera & Ballet Theatre on Nizami Street (p.93).

06 Eat At A Caravanserai

For a memorable experience of traditional Azeri dining, head to one of the caravanserai in Baku's Old City. Here friendly waiters will bring you plate after plate of delicious local food while the night air fills with strains of mugham music. See Karavan Saray, p.184, and Mugham Club, p.186.

Essentials

Baku Checklist

07 Buy A Carpet

Carpet making is one of Azerbaijan's proudest craft traditions, and you can shop for your own at the many stores in the Old City (see Shopping, p.130). There's a restriction on the age of the carpets you can take out of the country, so if you want to see some much older varieties head to the Carpet Museum (p.88).

Essentials

Baku Checklist

08 Take A Hamam
The luxury spa options are growing all the time with the imminent arrival of the half dozen new high-end hotels in Baku, but if you want a relaxation session that's a bit more old-school, try a soak and a scrub in one of the city's older hamams. It's a steamy experience like no other (see Spas, p.118).

09 Have A Tall Cocktail

There's a burgeoning rank of high-rollers in Baku, and there's no better place to get a slice of high society than from up high with a cocktail in hand. Try sipping on a Cosmopolitan at Sky Bar on the 19th floor of the Landmark Hotel, or on a Moscow Mule at the Mirvari Bar above the Park Inn (p.62); both have great views.

10 Stroll The Boulevard

The stretch of promenade between the city and the sea is where Bakuvians go to relax. The Boulevard is actually a national park and with cafes, fairground rides, a brand new mall and entertainment centre, and ubiquitous popcorn stalls, it's all going on, and is the perfect place for people watching. See p.72.

Best Of Baku

Essentials

For Architecture Buffs

Baku's differing styles of architecture are living evidence of the city's intriguing past. Buildings speak of the city's full history, from the medieval splendour of Shirvanshah's Palace (p.75) and narrow, winding streets of the Old City (p.74), to the iconic Maiden's Tower (p.78), the Soviet grandeur of the Dom Soviet building (p.16), and the 21st century transformation being brought to the capital by striking modern buildings such as the International Centre of Mugham (p.163) and the new crop of five-star hotels that are springing up.

For Big Spenders

If you've got cash to burn, and fashion is your middle name, Baku provides the perfect opportunity to fill up that spare suitcase with clothing from the glitzy boutiques along Neftchilar Prospect (see Fashion, p.140). Some good new malls are coming to town too, following in the path of Park Bulvar (p.152), and there's a classic Soviet department shop experience, MUM's, which should be ticked off every global shopper's list (p.146). Alternatively you can shop for something a little more traditional at one of the many carpet sellers' outlets in the Old City (p.74).

For Culture Vultures

There's some fascinating regional culture to be explored in Baku, from the informative at the History Museum (p.89) and Carpet Museum (p.88), art in the city's various galleries (p.84), traditional in the Museum of Azerbaijan Literature, and of course music – take your pick from jazz at the Jazz Centre (p.193), classical at the Opera & Ballet Theatre, or the unique mugham at the Mugham Club (p.186) or caravanserai restaurants (p.74).

For Foodies

A trip to Baku offers a great chance to sample some delicious Azeri food. Good places to try out the region's fresh flavours are Karavan Saray (p.184), Bah Bah (p.175), and Mugham Club (p.186). If you prefer to dine on international cuisine then there are plenty of other choices too, from Japanese at Zakura to German at Paul's. See Restaurants & Cafes, p.174.

For Party People

Baku is bouncing these days, and is starting to get a reputation as one of the region's party hotspots. Go for a sophisticated cocktail at a swanky venue with a view, such as Sky Bar at the Landmark Hotel (p.61), or tap into the bubbly expat scene at a venue like Finnegan's (p.197). Give your vocal chords a workout with some karaoke at Pride Karaoke Lounge (p.160), or get your clubbing gear on and join the local 'in crowd' at Face (p.197).

For Sports Fans

Azeris are sports mad and a trip to watch one of the national sports is a great experience; the two most popular sports are wrestling and football. Several teams from the recently formed Azerbaijan Premier League play in Baku and international matches are also held in the capital, p.126.

Visiting Baku

Essentials

Baku is accessible directly from many parts of Europe and the Middle East, but getting a visa is not so straight forward.

Getting There

Azerbaijan Airlines (Azal) is the national airline of Azerbaijan and flies to a surprisingly diverse list of locations across Europe and around the Middle East. Destinations operated include London, Paris, Milan, Moscow, St Petersburg, Tel Aviv and Dubai and the price is impressively competitive with many westerners using the airline.

BMI flies directly to Baku from the UK, while Austrian and Lufthansa also serve Azerbaijan from Europe. Tickets are not particularly cheap, though (economy class return to Heathrow on BMI costs from around $1,200) but these operators are perceived to be the most reliable, and their routes are busiest with European passengers.

Airport

The country's main airport is Heydar Aliyev International Airport (GYD). It has two terminals, but is very small and light on facilities. Work is underway on expanding and bringing the airport into the 21st century, and is rumoured to be set for completion by 2013.

Essentials

Turkish Airlines, which offers connections via Istanbul, is another excellent alternative for getting into Azerbaijan, while there is a whole host of smaller airlines operating directly from Baku (see table). These include the low-cost operator FlyDubai, which has opened up the whole of the UAE to Azerbaijan. Unfortunately, there are no direct flights from Baku to North America at the moment, but connections can be made via Europe.

Airlines

Aeroflot	012 498 1167	www.aeroflot.ru
Aerosvit Airlines	012 498 7119	www.aerosvit.ua
Air Astana	012 497 4996	www.airastana.com
Austrian Airlines	012 497 1822	www.austrianairlines.com
Azerbaijan Hava Yollari	012 598 8880	www.azal.az
Belavia	012 490 8162	www.en.belavia.by
BMI	012 497 0500	www.flybmi.com
British Airways	012 497 0500	www.britishairways.com
China Southern Airlines	na	www.flychinasouthern.com
FlyDubai	012 598 0598	www.flydubai.com
Iran Air	012 498 5886	www.iranair.com
Lufthansa	012 490 7050	www.lufthansa.com
Pulkovo	012 498 2930	www.pulkovo.ru
Scat Air Company	012 498 1918	www.scat.kz
Siberia Airlines	012 493 6774	www.s7.ru
Turkish Airlines	012 497 7300	www.turkishairlines.com
Utair Aviation	012 498 9141	www.utair.ru
Uzbekistan Airways	012 598 3120	www.uzairways.com

Airport Transfer

Unless you're being collected by either a hotel or a pre-arranged contact, taxi is your best way to get into Baku from the airport, and should cost between AZN15-20, depending on your powers of negotiation.

Visas & Customs

When it comes to visas, it's not a simple procedure for most nationalities to visit Azerbaijan – requirements are prone to sudden changes, so it always pays to check with your local embassy before you finalise your plans. There are three visa options to choose from: single entry (valid for between three and 90 days), double entry (valid for between three and 90 days) or transit (valid for up to five days). Until late 2010, certain nationalities were eligible to apply for a visa on arrival at Baku airport; however, a change in policy now means that all visitors to Azerbaijan, except Turkish and CIS nationals, must obtain a visa prior to arrival in the country.

To get one, you will require a Letter of Invitation (see p.34), which may need to be legalised by the Ministry of Foreign Affairs in Azerbaijan before it is accepted. You will also need two copies of the application form (available from the Ministry of Foreign Affairs in Baku or from your local Azerbaijani embassy), two passport photos, a passport valid for six months after the expiry date of the visa and a fee. Do not staple the photos to the application form as it will be rejected. Your local Azerbaijani embassy will be able to confirm how much the fee is, as it varies depending on the embassy and the nationality of the applicant.

Some embassies do not accept payments in cash, while others insist on cash payment, so be prepared for either. Applications take between three and 15 days to process and you may be required to attend an interview.

If you want to stay longer than 90 days, travelling in and out of the country freely, then you will need a Residency Permit which can only be applied for once you're in the country, so you will still need a visa for entry.

The duty free allowance on entry is 1,000 cigarettes or 1,000g of tobacco products, 1.5l of spirits or 2l of wine, a reasonable quantity of perfume for personal use and goods up to the value of $10,000. The import of weapons and narcotics is prohibited, as are live animals (except with the correct permit), fresh fruit or vegetables, or any anti-Azerbaijan propaganda materials.

Letter Of Invitation (LOI)

- **Invitation from an Azerbaijani company**
- **Invitation from a foreign company based in Azerbaijan**
- **Booking confirmation from a travel agency**
- **Hotel reservation confirmation**
- **Invitation from an Azerbaijani citizen with a copy of their passport or national identification card**
- **The LOI may have to be sent to the Ministry of Foreign Affairs in Baku to be stamped or 'legalised', which will require extra time and an additional fee**

Obtaining A Visa

New instructions from the Government authorities for Azerbaijan stress that tourists should now apply for their visas through tourist companies, who will apply to the consulates and embassies of the Republic of Azerbaijan within the applicant's home country, on their behalf.

These tourist companies will need to acquire and present the following – in electronic form – to the embassies and consulates of the Republic of Azerbaijan, in order to obtain the necessary visa:

- A completed application form taken from the website of embassies and consulates of the Republic of Azerbaijan
- A scanned copy of his/her photo
- A scanned copy of his/her passport
- A scanned copy of the receipt of the state fee
- A scanned copy of the documents confirming the tourist's purpose of visit including the passenger air flight ticket, a hotel reservation confirmation letter, and a letter confirming payment of the tourist services. The latter entitles the applicant to a reduced visa fee of $20. Prior to this service, visas could cost anywhere from $40 to $130 depending on the nationality

The processing time for each visa application should not take any longer than 15-20 working days. Embassies and consulates of the Republic of Azerbaijan will then issue an ordinary (single) entrance visa to individuals who are not exceeding a 30 day stay. If you receive an electronic visa, be sure to keep this safe, as it will not be attached in your passport. If your application is, for whatever reason, denied, you will be sent a letter stating the reasons for this rejection. These new rules will apply as of 1 June, 2011.

Dos & Don'ts

While Azerbaijan is tolerant and friendly, there are things to be aware of. Azeris are generally conservative in attitudes towards dress, especially outside Baku. Long trousers and a shirt are expected anywhere except the beach; women should avoid revealing or figure-hugging clothes, unless they are looking to attract a lot of attention. And although there are no real dress restrictions for women (other than not going out with wet hair or smoking in public – the behaviour of prostitutes apparently), men should avoid wearing shorts unless doing sport – this is regarded as tantamount to walking around in your underpants.

If you are offered a gift from someone, it is polite to refuse twice before accepting. Similarly, if you offer someone else a gift (or some petrol money after getting a lift somewhere), offer it three times before giving up. Three refusals suggests that you are definitely not willing to accept something. Azeris have a tendency to ask a lot of direct questions, so be prepared. You're also likely to find yourself on the receiving end of stares from Azeris, which are simply mannerisms of curiosity, nothing more. Smiling at people you don't know is not the done thing, neither is whistling in public, but a man should shake hands and say hello to every member of a group when meeting other men, even if they are strangers, but only shake a woman's hand if it is offered.

Essentials

Visiting Baku

Local Knowledge

Baku is a safe and friendly city where visitors from all over the world are warmly welcomed and offered insight into the exotic Azeri culture.

Climate

For a relatively small country, there is a great deal of variation in the climate in Azerbaijan. Famously boasting nine of the world's 11 climate zones within its borders, conditions range from hot and sub-tropical to cold and Alpine, so the weather you are likely to experience depends quite specifically on where you are and when you're there. Generally speaking though, much of Azerbaijan has a seasonal, Mediterranean-like climate – hot, dry summers and fairly mild winters in parts, particularly around Baku and along the Caspian shores.

In and around the capital, summer highs can reach the mid 30°C range, with high humidity making it a little uncomfortable in July and August. Winter lows in Baku can drop to around 5°C, but rarely lower than that, while rainfall tends to be highest in the spring. The most common adverse weather feature in the capital is the sporadic strong winds that whistle in off the Caspian.

Crime & Safety

Most tourists find Baku to be quite safe and manageable and there are no particularly dangerous neighbourhoods to be fearful of. Lately, anecdotal evidence has shown an increase in muggings and robberies, but no official statistic reflects this. Travelling by bus and metro is generally fine in terms of personal safety.

It's always wise to be cautious when travelling, taking precautions such as locking your valuables and important documents in your hotel safe, and keeping separate copies of your passport and visas.

Azerbaijan has a zero tolerance policy for driving under the influence of alcohol or drugs. Vehicles can be confiscated immediately in this instance. Penalties for minor hooliganism, or creating a non-violent public disturbance, range from an AZN20 penalty to 15 days of imprisonment. Major instances of violent disorder can lead to up to seven years in jail.

Contacting your embassy is the best course of action if you find yourself in trouble.

Police

In Azerbaijan, the police are formal and both receive and expect a certain level of respect from the public. Shaking hands (for men) and offering a polite greeting are both common ways to interact with a police officer, most of whom are uniformed and drive marked cars.

In case of an emergency that requires the assistance of the police, call 102. To summon police to road accidents or traffic emergencies, call 945. However, many people will advise you to avoid getting involved with police wherever possible, as systems are not always transparent and you may not get the results you expected.

Electricity & Water

The electricity supply in Azerbaijan is 220 volts, and most sockets are the European round two-pin plug variety. Grounding is not a uniformly standard practice so large appliances can deliver a nasty shock if they have not been properly installed; it certainly pays to be wary of faulty wiring in older premises. Contact an electrician or a member of the hotel staff should you be at all concerned.

The ground water supply in Baku is quite polluted, so drinking water directly from the tap is not recommended, although many locals continue to use it for cooking. Water is cleaner in the mountain regions outside the capital, but in Baku it would be much safer to buy bottled mineral water, that can be found for 50 qepik per litre in all of the local shops and supermarkets.

Female Visitors

For women, being in Baku requires no more vigilance than any other city other city around the world and generally speaking, common sense rules apply. You may wish to consider carrying a small flashlight, as streets are not well lit at night, and also be aware that young women out alone at night can be mistaken for prostitutes. Ignoring any chiding and walking with purpose is usually enough to stop any forms of harassment.

Women in Baku are not expected to cover up, unlike in some stricter Muslim countries, but some places, such as tea houses and hamams, are male-dominated and should probably be avoided.

Essentials

Local Knowledge

Language

Azeri is the nation's official tongue, and is a language from the Turkic family. It is also possible to converse fairly easily if you speak Russian. English is less common in much of the country; some people in Baku will speak it, but not all, while out of the main cities it is rarely used. Knowing some useful everyday phrases will help a great deal, particularly when dealing with taxi drivers and in restaurants.

Basic Azeri

General

Yes	Ha (familiar) Bali (formal)
No	Yokh; Kheyr
Please	Lutfan
Thank you (very much)	(Chok) Sag ol
God willing	Inshallah

Questions

How many?	Necha dana?
How much?	Na gadar?
Where?	Harada?
When?	Na vakht?
Which?	Hansi?
What?	Na?
Why?	Niya?
Who?	Kim?
And	Va
Please take me to…	Zahmat olmasa, mani… aparin.
Stop	Sakhla

Greetings

Hello	Salam aleykum
How are you?	Nejasan?
(Very) well thank you	Sag ol, (chok) yakshi
Good Morning	Sabahin(iz)* kheyir
Good Afternoon	Gunortan(iz)* kheyir
Good Evening	Akshamin(iz)* kheyir
Good Night	Gejän(iz)* kheyir
Goodbye	Sag ol or Khudahafiz

*(iz) is added for formal situations

Introduction

My name is…	Adim … dir
What is your name?	Adiniz nädir?
Where are you from?	Siz haradansiniz?

Numbers

Zero	Sifr
One	bir
Two	iki
Three	üch
Four	dörd
Five	besh
Six	alti
Seven	yeddi
Eight	sakkiz
Nine	dogguz
Ten	on
Hundred	yüz
Thousand	min

The Extra Letters

There are several 'extra' letters in the Azeri alphabet. You may see them written in their Azeri style in literature and signs, or with a Roman equivalent (as is mainly the case in this book), or a combination of both. Ç is written as ch; ə is similar to a short 'a'; ğ is written as 'gh', and sounds like the rolling French 'r'. X and kh are interchangeable in written form, but sound like a hard 'kh'; ı is usually written consistently (like a small capital I), but the pronunciation should be more like 'y'. Ö can be written as 'er', ş as 'sh', and ü as 'ew'. There's no w, and a few familiar-looking letters have a different sound: 'c' is said like a soft 'j', 'g' is 'gy' or 'gya', 'j' like 'zh' or 'shja', and 'q' is a hard 'g'.

Money

Azerbaijan's currency is the manat, or 'new manat', which is represented by the ₼ symbol, but is commonly abbreviated to AZN or man. One manat is divided into 100 qepik, and the notes in circulation are AZN1 (grey), AZN5 (orange), AZN10 (blue), AZN20 (green), AZN50 (yellow), and AZN100 (purple). The front of each note features an image of significance from Azeri culture (such as musical instruments on the AZN1 note or a map of Baku's Old City on the AZN10 note), while the reverse side has a silhouette of the shape of the country. Coins are 1, 3, 5, 10, 20 and 50 qepik.

Essentially Azerbaijan is a cash-only society. Around Baku you'll see the usual credit card signs on shop doors, but the machines rarely work, even in big brand stores. Notable exceptions are the Citimart and New World supermarkets, the expensive restaurants and the larger hotels. Fortunately there are lots of ATMs around Baku, so getting hold of cash in the capital is no problem.

People With Disabilities

Baku is not an easy place to be if you have a disability, and there seems to be a general lack of awareness and understanding about the challenges faced by disabled residents and visitors. There are few pavements and lots of steps, which makes wheelchairs (and pushchairs) almost impossible to use in the city. Although there are ramps on the stairs in all of the new parks, these have been designed for pushchairs and would be too steep to tackle in a wheelchair. Toilets with wide doors and support rails are conspicuous by their absence, as are parking spaces reserved for disabled drivers. Even in very new buildings the absence of facilities is apparent.

Telephone & Internet

There's no shortage of mobile phone options in Baku, and you'll find stores selling phones and phone packages on virtually every block. The big names are Azercell, Bakcell and Nar Mobile. Azercell is known for having the most comprehensive coverage countrywide, but in Baku all things are equal.

Anyone with an active visa and local address (such as your hotel's address) can purchase a phone and local number. You'll need to buy a phone number along with your first phone, and you can pay for call card refills as needed. Prices of phone numbers vary depending on popularity. The cheapest phone numbers can cost just AZN15, but those considered lucky or easy to remember could cost hundreds of manat.

Wi-Fi is available in cafes across town and in most hotels, and it's hard to walk a city block without running into an internet cafe or club. Charges are AZN1 per hour on average. After school hours, hoards of teenage boys flock to play games and surf the internet, so things can get crowded quickly. Most cafes in the Fountain Square area offer Wi-Fi, and some good spots to relax with free Wi-Fi are Aroma Café near the Sahil metro (p.175), Chocolate Café in the Old City (p.74) and Café Caramel (p.176) and Café Mozart (p.176) off Fountain Square.

If you need internet on the move, there are a number of mobile internet providers offering 3mb speed. These include: Elcell (39 Khagani Street, 012 598 2021, www.elcell.az) and Azerfon (18 Azadliq Avenue, 012 444 0788, www.azerfon.az).

Time

Azerbaijan is four hours ahead of UTC (Co-ordinated Universal Time, also known as GMT). Clocks are altered for daylight saving, when the time is shifted forward an hour, and changes occur

Roam From Home

If you are using your own phone from your home country while in Baku, make sure you check with your provider what the charges for data roaming are, or you could face a nasty surprise when you return home.

A view over the Icheri Sheher

on the same schedule as UTC (usually going forward on the last Sunday in March and back on the last Sunday in October).

Tipping

Tipping is not a hard and fast practice in Azerbaijan as it is in the US and parts of Europe. If you want to leave a tip for a waiter in a restaurant, somewhere between 5% and 10% of the bill is a good range, but it's never usually obligatory. Tipping taxi drivers is not necessary, as ideally you will have agreed a fee before setting off to your destination.

Media & Further Reading

As Baku continues its transformation into a model modern metropolis there are more and more ways of keeping informed and entertained.

Newspapers & Magazines

There are several free English language newspapers, such as the *Caspian Business News*, *Baku Sun* and the *Azeri Times*, which are published weekly and are available from outlets around the city. These publications offer brief international news and local interest articles, along with a large selection of listings and classifieds.

The English language *magAZine* (commonly called *AZ Mag*) is Baku's answer to *Hello!* for the expat community. For a more highbrow outlook on Azeri culture, *Azerbaijan International* is a respected independent publication with a thorough website (www.azer.com).

There are a number of imported titles available in supermarkets, but these will usually be several days old and come with a hefty price tag, usually in excess of AZN5. The higher-end hotels provide international newspapers for guests.

The national and local press (both Russian and Azeri language) is an unswervingly patriotic, pro-government affair. Some publications cover current events, others cover sports, others still cover financials and there are various classifieds papers for cars and property. Newspapers are sold at kiosks, by street vendors and at metro stations. The main titles are:

Bizim Asr, Yeni Musavat, Yeni Azerbaycan, Xalq Cebhesi, Echo and *Zerkalo*.

The best option for finding information on events and entertainment in the city is to look online at sites like www.citylife.az and www.bakuguide.az.

Television

Most decent hotels provide in-room satellite TV, with the range of channels including the local Azeri selection, Turkish and Russian language services, and English channels coming from the Middle East, India and Africa. One or all of CNN, BBC World News and Euro News may be shown, in addition to channels like MTV, VH1, Eurosport, ESPN, Hallmark, Nickelodeon, National Geographic and Discovery, and there will be a small selection of movie channels.

Radio

Most radio stations in Azerbaijan play a mix of pop and jazz with adverts, news and talk radio thrown in for good measure. The pop music is usually a mix of 80s and 90s American and European hits, along with catchy Azeri and Turkish tunes. There are many popular stations, including ANS Radio (102FM, www.ansradio.ws), Burç FM (100.5FM, www.burc.fm), Radio Space (104FM, www.spacetv.az), Azad FM (106FM), Lider Jazz Radio (107FM, www.lidertv.com), and Mugam Radio (www.mugamradio.az). International radio stations are banned from broadcasting on national frequencies in Azerbaijan, so English language radio services are only available online.

Public Holidays & Annual Events

Party with the locals at one of the major annual events for the best insight into local culture and traditions.

There is a generous amount of national public holidays in Azerbaijan (see table). Causes for celebration include a mix of Islamic festivals, national events, Soviet legacy, and Gregorian calendar highlights. Although Friday is the Muslim holy day, weekends are typically taken over Saturday and Sunday.

Both Eid Al Fitr and Eid Al Adha are celebrated with two days off, and there are a number of public holidays that mark significant events in Azerbaijan's independent history, including Heydar Aliyev's Birthday, Republic Day, and National Independence Day. One of the biggest holidays is Novruz Bayram, a five-day celebration of spring and the New Year that has its roots in the ancient religion of Zoroastrianism.

Opening Hours

The working week in Baku follows the standard European Monday to Friday, rather than the Middle Eastern Sunday to Thursday. Hours of operation for most businesses are 09:00 to 17:00, but shops generally stay open until later, while restaurants and bars keep serving until at least 23:00 – later if business is going well.

Public Holidays

New Year	1 & 2 January (fixed)
Martyr's Day	20 January (fixed)
Women's Day	8 March (fixed)
Novruz Bayram	20-24 March 2012 (equinox)
Victory Day	9 May (fixed)
Heydar Aliyev's Birthday	10 May (fixed)
Republic Day	28 May (fixed)
National Salvation Day	15 June (fixed)
Armed Forces Day	26 June (fixed)
National Independence Day	18 October (fixed)
Constitution Day	12 November (fixed)
Day of National Revival	17 November (fixed)
International Solidarity Day of Azerbaijanis	31 December (fixed)
Ramazam Bayram (Eid Al Fitr)	30-31 August 2011; 19-20 August 2012 (moon)
Gurban Bayram (Eid Al Adha)	6-7 November 2011; 25-26 October 2012 (moon)

Annual Events

Baku boasts a few key events that draw the crowds each year. The Jazz Festival has been going for several years, and took place in 2010 in October (although the month has a tendency to shift). The opera and ballet season runs from October to June (see p.164), while people from the energy industry come to town for the Caspian Oil & Gas Conference each June.

Getting Around

Baku may be congested and the roads a little daunting, but with a little preparation it's not too hard to get around town.

Baku is a sprawling city and it takes most people a little while to become familiar with it. Like in the USA and Europe, Azerbaijan's road users drive on the right, although you may wonder if anyone knows this, as locals merrily motor down both sides, and the congestion can be stifling. Luckily for visitors, Baku has a comprehensive public transport system of buses, minibuses (*marshrutka*), taxis and a metro. There's even a funicular railway at the western end of the Boulevard. The metro has been undergoing improvements for a few years and the network continues to expand to service this growing city.

Bus

There is a vast fleet of buses on the road in Baku, and they come in all sizes and states of repair; some incredibly ancient vehicles are still in service but showing their age, and they are generally crammed with as many passengers as possible (women will always get a seat, however). Modernisation is in progress; a new bus station was opened in 2009, and in 2010 a huge new fleet of buses was introduced.

The buses go everywhere, and fares are cheap – 20 qepik per ride, no matter how far. If you change buses, you simply pay again; there is no travel card system and you'll need exact change. There seems to be no timetable either, but buses reliably run right through the day, from early in the morning (05:00 or 06:00) until around midnight, with a frequency of around five minutes.

Bus stops are visible in some places (you'll see people waiting at them) but you can just hail a bus anywhere, hop on and let the driver know when you want to get off again. The most confusing aspect is figuring out exactly where each bus goes. Destinations are usually displayed on a board in the window, but the names used are not consistent; one bus might display an old (Soviet era) name, and the next will use the new name. Routes are also changeable depending on road congestion and closure. They can be somewhat confusing at first, but are an undeniably atmospheric means of travel.

Marshrutkas are little minibuses and are used a bit like large taxis. You can hail them from anywhere and pay as you get off. They cost a little more than a standard bus but are usually quicker, as the drivers tend to be quite reckless.

Useful Phrases

Please could you tell me the name of this station? Bu hansi stansiyadir?

Where can I buy a travel card? Uzr isteyirem, bileti hardan almag olar?

When is the last train to...? Akhringi gatar ne vakht gedir?

Straight on Duz
Left Sola (sol la)
Right Sağa
Here Burada
How much? Nechayadir?

www.liveworkexplore.com

Metro

The metro is often the quickest way from A to B, provided your destination is close to a station. The metro system was initiated by the Soviets at the end of the 1960s, and the first seven stations were placed deep underground to double as bomb shelters while the Cold War threat was imminent.

It remains in pretty good working order, it's clean and, in terms of personal safety, it is probably as safe as the metro of any other capital city. Trains run every five minutes or so, from 06:00 to 01:00, and cover most of the central areas of Baku (see map, Inside front cover).

Travel cards can be purchased at stations for AZN2 (refundable when you hand them back). These are then 'charged' with money for fares. Fares are 15 qepik per journey. It helps to know some basic Russian or Azeri, as there are practically no signs and the station names are not visible from on board. The best advice is to count the number of stops you want to make before you board the train.

Train

If you want to explore beyond Baku, you can use the rail network to visit almost all of Azerbaijan's major towns; you can even take a sleeper service overnight to neighbouring Georgia. The journeys are extremely slow but they're also very cheap. A first-class ticket to Tbilisi is around $50, and second-class costs about half that. You can buy tickets at Baku central station on Azadlig Prospect. If you don't speak any Azeri or Russian, take someone with you to translate and make sure you have your passport.

Funicular

The funicular runs from the western end of the Boulevard (next to Chinar restaurant) up to Martyrs' Alley at the top of the hill overlooking Bayil. The beautiful Turkish Mosque (no longer operating as a mosque) is close to the top station and well worth a visit. Journeys on the funicular cost 20 qepik each way and take less than five minutes.

Taxi

Taxis are readily available across the city and, although unmetered, can be relatively cheap if you negotiate. A typical journey across Downtown should cost no more than AZN5, but can be as little as AZN3 if you speak some Russian or Azeri. Cabs to the airport are usually around AZN20, but more expensive on the way back into the city. Licensed cabs have blue number plates, but the majority of taxis are unlicensed.

If you are out and about at night, you'll easily find a taxi on Nizami Street, around the expat bars of Alizadeh (Abdulkarrim Alizadeh Street) and Rasul Rza and around Fountain Square. It's possible to find a cab in the post-party early-morning hours, even outside the Downtown area.

> **Taxi Tips**
> When taking a cab, it's helpful to be able to give directions in Azeri:
> **Straight on:** Duz
> **Left:** Sola (sol lar)
> **Right:** Sağa (sagha)
> **This building:** Bu bina
> **Here:** Burada
> **How much?** Neçəyədir? (Nechayadir)

Many taxi drivers don't know the names of streets, due to their frequent name changes, so it's best to give your driver a landmark (park, metro station, hotel or other well-known building) to navigate by. Taxis will honk their horns or flash their lights to let you know they're available for hire. You can flag them down anywhere, but negotiate before you get in, as drivers tend to hike the price when they're dropping you off. Tipping is becoming more commonplace, although it was not expected in the past.

Most cabs are Ladas or similar, and drivers will try to take as many people as they can fit in. Bear in mind that there are unlikely to be any seatbelts and driving will be erratic at best. If you smell propane, get out of the cab; since the recent hike in petrol prices, some taxis have been rigged to run on propane gas cylinders, which have been known to explode.

If you want to order a taxi, try calling Taxi-Service (012 437 9999) or SA Company (012 437 8898).

Walking

If you are staying in the Downtown area, walking is the quickest method of getting around, and is the best way to get a close up look at Baku (especially the Old City). There's very little in the way of street crime in Baku, so travelling on foot is a pretty safe option, although pavements are a bit of an issue as, when present, they tend to be in a poor state of repair.

Crossing main roads is also fraught with danger, so take care; drivers treat pedestrian crossings as more of a suggestion that they can stop if they wish than an actual command to do so.

Hiring a Car

To hire a car in Baku, all you need is your international driver's licence and a lot of courage. Baku's roads come in every shape, size and state, from the smooth, multi-lane Neftchilar Prospect along the Boulevard, to the tiny little higgledy-piggledy lanes around Teza Bazaar in Kubinka. Often roads are potholed or have gaping holes where manhole covers used to be, and there's little in the way of lane discipline; you'll often see five cars across three marked lanes, and drivers constantly swerve in and out of traffic in an effort to get to their destination quicker. Baku's one-way systems can be infuriating and often require you to drive around most of the city centre to get from one side to the other. If you do decide to get behind the wheel, prices for car hire vary from AZN50 to AZN80 per day and you can add a personal driver for a small additional fee.

Car Rental Agencies

Avis	012 497 5455	www.avis.az
Car & Country	012 437 9432	www.rentacar.az
Caspian Car Hire	012 490 5102	www.cic.az
Express Service System (ESS)	012 511 7060	www.ess.az
Hertz	012 497 8757	www.hertz.com
Hestia	012 418 7681	www.hestia.az
Orient Express	012 514 2136	www.orientexpress.az
RAM Servis	012 511 3244	www.ramservis.az

www.liveworkexplore.com

Places To Stay

Essentials

Baku's range of top hotels is about to increase dramatically, but in the meantime there are some reliable options to choose from.

Baku Hotels

For a capital city, Baku has, until now, been somewhat lacking in the provision of top-end hotels, but a recent rush among the big-name chains to get a foothold in the capital is set to change all that. Construction is underway in the centre of town with plans for a Hilton, a JW Marriott, a Four Seasons, a Kempinski, a Dedeman and a Fairmont, among others. Until then, the two Hyatts (see below) probably offer the best option if you're looking for a touch of luxury. Some of the standout hotel options are briefly highlighted below, as well as a selection of smaller, comfortable boutique places. There is also a wide range of low to medium-range venues that offer rooms and basic facilities for a lower price; for a comprehensive list see www.azerbaijan.tourism.az.

Ambassador Hotel
www.hotelambassador.az　　　　　　　　　　012 449 4930

This sizeable, upper-end hotel is popular with business travellers. Facilities include an all-day dining restaurant, a roof-top bar, a good-sized indoor swimming pool, and a gym. Convenient for business headquarters in the Ganjlik area.
Map 1 C4

Essentials

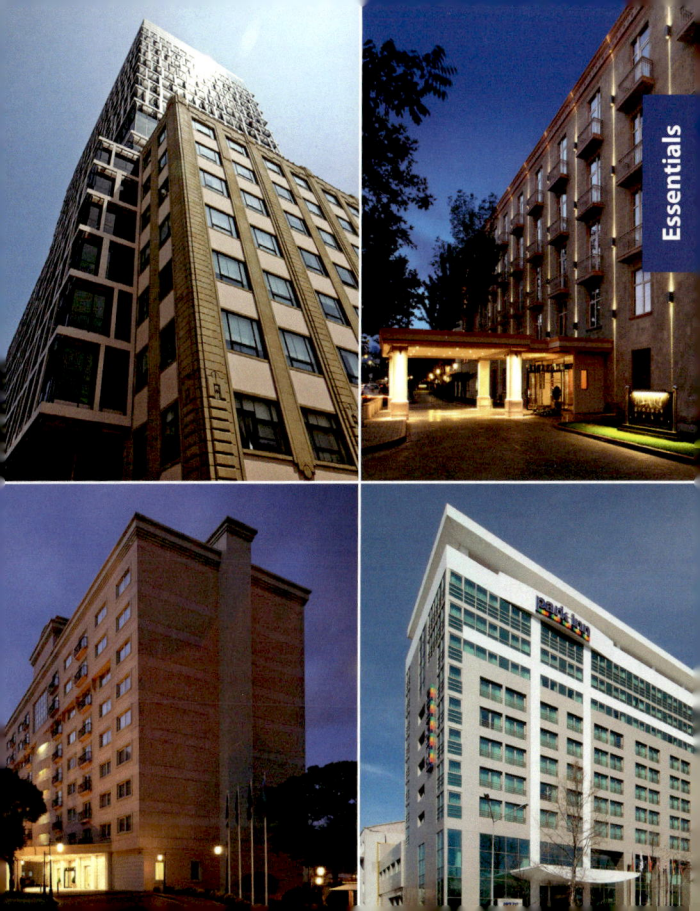

Essentials

Places To Stay

Austin Hotel
www.austinhotel.az　　　　　　　　　　　　　012 598 0812
A small but smart boutique option in the heart of Downtown. All 31 rooms have balconies offering a vantage point over the bustling Baku streets, breakfast is included, and there are business facilities and a fitness centre. **Map** 2 E5 **Metro** Sahil

Azcot
www.azcothotel.com　　　　　　　　　　　　012 492 5477
Azcot is a decent hotel occupying a 19th century mansion downtown. It's not the most extravagant place in town, but the rooms are comfortable and the decor is refined, and there are multiple choices for eating out in the immediate area. **Map** 2E5 **Metro** Sahil

Boutique Palace
www.boutique-palace.com　　　　　　　　　012 492 2288
Although it doesn't quite live up to the self-styled 'boutique' tag, this hotel is quite comfortable, if somewhat over-priced. Location is its main draw, as it abuts an area of the ancient ramparts of the Old City. **Map** 2 E5 **Metro** Icheri Sheher

Excelsior Hotel Baku
www.excelsiorhotelbaku.az　　　　　　　　012 496 8000
This is Baku's grandest hotel, just out of the city centre, and a favourite of the wealthy set. It's a plush affair, and features an amazing indoor swimming pool, complete with a running track, as well as an outdoor pool and the Aura Wellness Centre spa (p.119). **Map** 2 J2 **Metro** Narimanov or Khatai

Grand Hotel Europe

www.grand-europe.com　　　　　　　　　　012 490 7090
The Grand is still at the higher end in terms of price, but the facilities are now a little dated compared to the newer hotels. It has a fitness centre, two pools, and a nightclub, Capone's.
Map 2 C1 **Metro** 20 Yanvar

Hyatt Regency Baku

www.baku.regency.hyatt.com　　　　　　　012 496 1234
Along with the neighbouring Park Hyatt, the Regency has for some time been the main hotel in town. The shared complex features a number of popular bars and restaurants (see Park Hyatt, p.62), and rooms in both hotels are of a high standard.
Map 2 D2 **Metro** Nizami

Landmark Hotel Baku

www.thelandmarkhotel.az　　　　　　　　　012 465 2000
This standout hotel in the heart of the city has good-sized rooms and a 10th floor swimming pool. The Sky Bar (p.202) on the 19th floor serves up cocktails with amazing views, and there's also a sushi bar (Seto) and an Asian restaurant (Shin Shin). **Map** 2 G4 **Metro** 28th of May

Old City Inn

www.oldcityinn.com　　　　　　　　　　　012 497 4369
A small but friendly option right in the Old City, this characterful hotel has just 12 rooms. There are great views from the rooftop, where there's a cafe, while dining choices in the vicinity are plentiful. **Map** 2 E5 **Metro** Icheri Sheher

Park Hyatt Baku

www.baku.hyatt.com   012 490 1234

The Park Hyatt is a five-star business hotel that shares facilities with the adjacent Regency. Dining options include the Mediterranean Mezzo restaurant and The Grill (p.182), while the Britannia Pub (p.194) and Beluga Bar (p.193) are popular drinking spots. **Map** 2 D2 **Metro** Nizami

Park Inn Hotel Azerbaijan

www.parkinn.com   012 490 6000

Located opposite the Boulevard and overlooking the Caspian Sea, the Park Inn is a solid four-star option. Rooms are comfortable, and there's a good sushi and cocktail bar, Mirvari, that affords great views. **Map** 2 F5 **Metro** Sahil

Radisson Blu Plaza Hotel

www.radissonblu.com/hotel-baku   012 498 2402

The Radisson Blu overlooks Fountain Square, and occupies the top floors of the high-rise ISR Plaza building. The studio-like suites offer excellent views over the heart of the capital, and there's a good cocktail bar, City Lights (p.194), with a spectacular panorama. **Map** 2 E5 **Metro** Sahil or Icheri Sheher

Sultan Inn Boutique Hotel

www.sultaninn.com   012 437 2308

Probably the most attractive Old City option, this is a luxury boutique hotel with 11 well-appointed rooms. The rooftop bar (p.202) is a great spot for a cocktail overlooking Maiden's Tower. **Map** 2 E6 **Metro** Icheri Sheher

Essentials

Places To Stay

Beach Hotels

Baku may not have the glorious city beaches of, say, Rio or Dubai, but there are a couple of noteworthy nearby stretches of sand.

There are big beach resorts spread along the shores of the Caspian, within easy reach of Baku and popular both for overnight stays and for day trips to enjoy the facilities. Shikhov (or Shikh) Beach is only a few kilometres south from the city centre. Slightly further away on the north coast of the Absheron Peninsula are the Novkhani beaches.

AF Hotel Aqua Park
www.afhotel.az　　　　　　　　　　　　　　　　012 448 3030
A 20km drive south of Baku at Novkhani, this is home to the popular Aqua Park. Featuring numerous swimming pools and slides, and private beach access, the leisure facilities even include an ice rink. Accommodation is in fairly standard hotel rooms and self-catering suites.

Crescent Beach Hotel & Leisure Resort
www.cbh.az　　　　　　　　　　　　　　　　　012 497 4777
Directly next door to the Ramada at Shikhov Beach, the Crescent Beach Hotel & Leisure Resort offers a pool, sauna and 400 metres of private beach. Rooms are standard but comfortable, and day access to the beach facilities is available to day visitors. **Map** 1 B7

Khazar Golden Beach Hotel & Resort
www.khazarbeachhotel.com 012 554 0710
This four-star establishment on Sahil Beach is a popular alternative to the Shikhov resorts with a stretch of private beach, swimming pools and a popular pub.

Ramada Baku
www.ramada.com 012 491 7303
Located 8km south of Baku on Shikhov Beach, the Ramada has comprehensive facilities, including a private beach with watersports, a night club, two restaurants and a bar. **Map** 1 B7

Essentials

Exploring

Explore Baku	68
At A Glance	70
The Boulevard	72
Old City (Icheri Sheher)	74
Downtown Baku	80
Around The City	82
Art Galleries	84
Museums	88
Theatres & Entertainment Venues	92
Parks, Beaches & Attractions	96
Tours & Sightseeing	102
Further Out	104

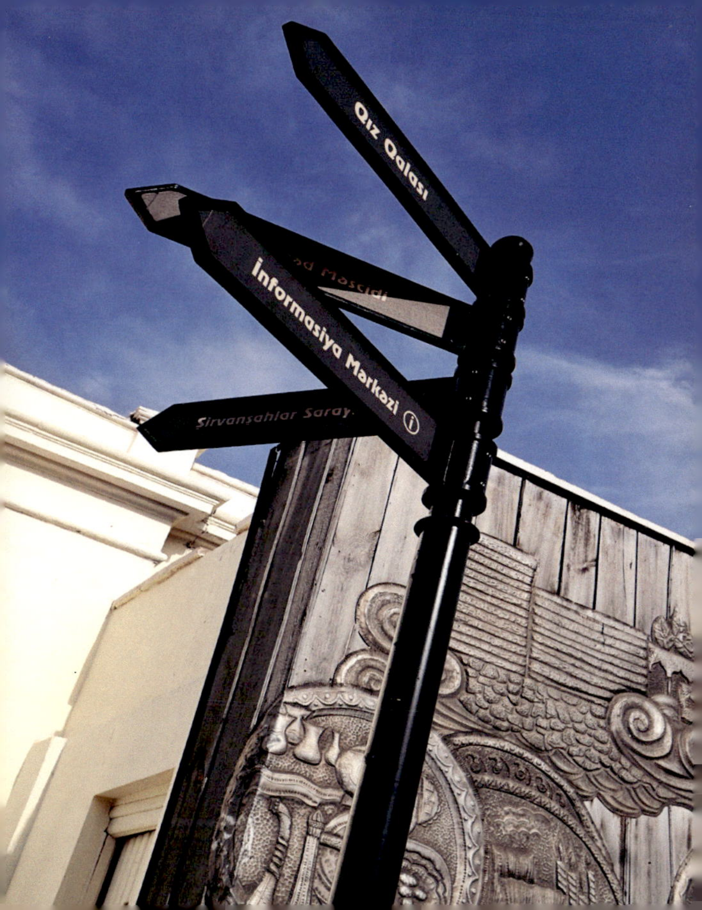
Qız Qalası
İnformasiya Mərkəzi
Şirvanşahlar Saray

Explore Baku

Add a touch of east and a dash of west, throw in a large dose of old and a heavy sprinkling of new; there's a little bit of everything to enjoy in Baku.

Modern Baku is a densely packed cosmopolitan city of some two million people, and it's a dynamic mixture of east, west, Soviet, European, Middle Eastern, ancient and current; you're as likely to hear pulsing techno as often as traditional mugham music. There's also a strong sense of impermanence; things come and go rapidly, businesses open and close, names and phone numbers change and prices are ever-increasing, while construction seems to be one of the few constants.

The city's development has been driven by the 20th and 21st century's insatiable appetite for oil, but the ancient traditions of this part of the world still hold their own against encroaching modern growth. The Old City, along with Shirvanshah's Palace and Maiden's Tower, are on the UNESCO World Heritage Site list, while mugham music, which can be heard at caravanserais and cultural centres around the city, has also been recognised by UNESCO. There's fun of every kind to be had all over town though, with dozens of galleries, museums, parks and entertainment venues for visitors to enjoy.

To get your bearings in the Azerbaijani capital, imagine being on a boat just outside the crescent-shaped Baku harbour, looking north to the city. From here, the city looks like a hodgepodge of buildings and green spots, spreading upwards like an amphitheatre. The Boulevard (p.170) juts out into the sea, a bit like the apron of a stage. To the left of the city is a hill so steep that few buildings cling to it. A small strip of flat land forms the eastern mouth of the harbour, curving around the bottom of the hill. To the right of the centre are the remains of the ugly infrastructure of the oil industry, which follow the curve of the harbour all the way to the eastern end of the harbour mouth.

Most of Baku was built in three main architectural styles – ancient and medieval, oil-boom European (1880-1920) and Soviet (1920-1991). The medieval period's near-circular Old City (p.170) makes up the inner core, while the elegant mansions of the oil boom period form the outer city. Soviet style buildings form a third zone that extends for many kilometres.

Sleek, modern buildings are increasingly found randomly throughout the city and the government has made a deliberate shift in architectural styles to distinguish Baku from other Caucasian cities and establish the place as a 'new Dubai'. While the entire city covers a relatively large area, many tourist spots are within walking distance of each other, in and around the Downtown area.

Baku really is a city that is best explored on foot and there are ample opportunities for catching both the atmospheric history of the place and the fast paced embracing of the modern world.

Exploring

At A Glance

Heritage Sites

Shirvanshah's Palace	p.75
Maiden's Tower	p.78

Museums & Art Galleries

Absheron Gallery	p.84
Ali Shamshir's Gallery	p.84
Art Gallery Vitru	p.85
The Azerbaijan State Museum Of Art	p.85
Carpet Museum, Theatre Museum & Museum Of Independence	p.88
Centre For Contemporary Art	p.85
History Museum	p.89
Miniature Book Museum	p.90
Museum Of Modern Art	p.86
Nizami Museum Of Azerbaijan Literature	p.90
Qiz Qalasi Gallery	p.86
Yusif Mirza's Studio	p.86

Parks, Beaches & Attractions

Botanical Gardens	p.96
Heydar Aliyev Park	p.97
Huseyn Javid Park	p.97
Khagani Park	p.98
Martyrs' Alley	p.98
Sahil Park	p.100
Zorge Park	p.100

Theatres & Entertainment Venues

Azerbaijan State Philharmonia	p.94
Azerbaijan State Puppet Theatre	p.92
Heydar Aliyev Palace	p.92
Musical Comedy Theatre	p.93
Opera & Ballet Theatre	p.93

Exploring

Exploring: The Boulevard

The Boulevard is a national institution (officially it's classed as a national park) and when the weather's half decent it thrums with life.

Also referred to as the Corniche or Caspian Waterfront, the Boulevard is a three-kilometre promenade which runs along the seafront, and its many trees, cafes, fountains and amusement park rides provide a lovely backdrop for strolling along the waterfront. Locals come in families, couples and groups to spend their relaxation time walking up and down this stretch, and it's a great place for people watching.

There's plenty to see and do along the length of the Boulevard too. At the Old City end stands one of the world's highest flagpoles, a musical fountain, and the International Centre of Mugham (p.12). A little way eastwards, opposite Maiden's Tower, is the Puppet Theatre (p.92), then if you wander further along you'll see two of Baku's grander neoclassical buildings – first, the Museum Centre (p.144), and a few blocks later, the huge Government House. In between these two, on the promenade, you'll find the brand new Park Bulvar mall (p.152), which is home to some upmarket shops and family entertainment options, while all the way along the esplanade are stalls selling snacks and street food, alfresco cafes and fairground rides, including carousels, bumper cars and a Ferris wheel.

Government House

Exploring

The Boulevard

Exploring

Old City (Icheri Sheher)

The Old City is Baku's standout visitor attraction, and is one of UNESCO's celebrated World Heritage Sites.

It's a living monument to Baku's centuries-old heritage, and is as much a vibrant place of enterprise, art and life as it is a heritage site. Surrounded by ancient city walls, the winding alleyways and higgledy-piggledy buildings of this medieval enclave within the modern metropolis ooze charm and atmosphere. You could spend several hours meandering the cobblestone streets to see what you stumble across, but there are also a number of worthy attractions to actively seek out.

The Old City's ancient monuments include Maiden's Tower (p.78), the fortress walls and towers (which date back to the 11th and

Caravanserais

Caravanserais were resting places for both people and animals in travelling caravans, and usually had an open interior courtyard with small rooms around the outside, with thick stone walls and limited entrances as defence against thieves. Some of Baku's historic caravanserais within the inner city have been turned into restaurants, including the atmospheric Karavan Saray (p.184) and the Mugham Club (p.186).

12th centuries) and Shirvanshah's Palace (p.75). Its oldest parts date back to the seventh century and reconstruction is ongoing.

The best way to appreciate the Old City is to simply wander through the labyrinth of alleyways on foot. The Double Gate area, near Fountain Square, is a good place to start. As you pass through the walls, turning right will take you towards the Shirvanshah's Palace (p.75), while wandering down the hill, heading in a southerly direction, will bring you to Maiden's Tower (p.78).

Head in either direction and you're likely to hear traditional Azeri mugham music playing, along with the click and slap of dice being thrown by men huddled along the street playing *nard* (Russian backgammon); you'll probably also smell the delicious aroma of cooking *shashlik* (barbecued lamb kebabs). You'll stumble across multiple carpet sellers too, whose wares add splashes of colour to the neutral earth tones of the walls and buildings.

There are a number of interesting art studios and galleries here (p.84). You can find refreshment in some atmospheric caravanserais, and there are several old bathhouses, or hamams, such as the Haji-Bani Bathhouse (16th century) near Maiden's Tower.

Shirvanshah's Palace   012 492 1073
4 Boyuk Gala St, Old City

There are few signs to indicate what lies behind the tan-coloured walls of Shirvanshah's Palace and, while it's not as large or ornate as some other palaces, it's nevertheless a striking place and well worth visiting. The view of the curved, coloured walls set against the Caspian Sea is very photogenic, particularly at sunset.

The complex is named after the Shirvanshahs, who ruled the state of Shirvan in northern Azerbaijan from the sixth to the 16th centuries, and it is one of the most extensive and impressive examples of traditional Azeri architecture. It contains a two-storey palace with 25 rooms on the first floor and 27 on the second.

Other buildings in the complex include a burial vault for the ruling family, a mosque with a minaret, the octagonal-shaped *divankhana* or main audience room, the mausoleum of Seyid Yahya Bakuvi (a famous astronomer of the time), Murad's gate and a bathhouse.

Entry to Shirvanshah Palace complex costs AZN2, plus an additional AZN2 to use your camera. It's open from 10:00 to 17:00 daily, and is rarely crowded. Some of the main building is closed off, and a private collection of metalware from ancient times occupies much of the open part of the main palace; admission to this costs AZN10.

> **A Place Of Note**
> The palace is depicted on the AZN10 banknote and its striking architectural features include the mosque's minaret, which is 22 metres tall, and the courtyard's large stone carved blocks, relocated from a fortress now submerged by the Caspian.
> Map 2 J10
> Metro Icheri Sheher

Exploring

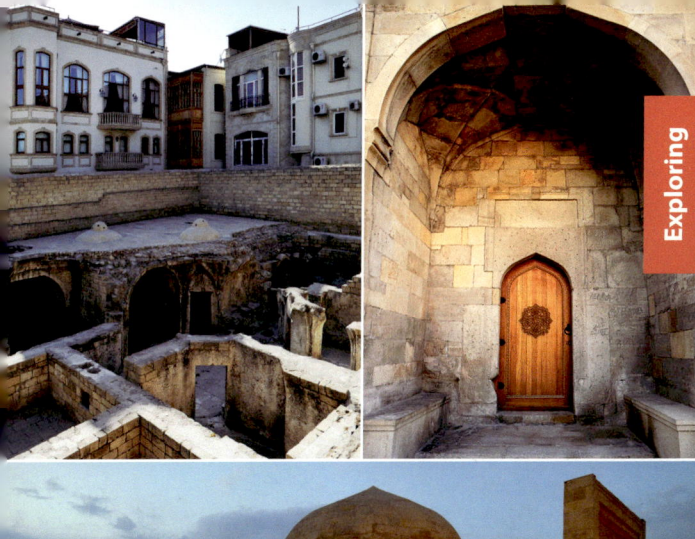

Maiden's Tower
012 492 8304
Neftchilar Ave, Old City

London has Big Ben, Paris the Eiffel Tower and Baku has the Maiden's Tower, or 'Qiz Qalasi'; this major tourist attraction is also the symbol of Azerbaijan. The castle-like structure sits between the Boulevard and the Old City, and its architecture and presence are remarkable.

It stands around 16 metres wide and eight levels high, and estimated dates of construction of different sections are put at between the seventh and 12th century AD. It's possible to climb right to the top (for an AZN2 fee), up seven sets of steep, uneven rock stairs. At the top of each staircase are circular rooms with exhibits and there's a photo studio where you can try on traditional Azeri costumes, and have your photo taken. From the top, the views are spectacular, and well worth the climb, but brace yourself for the strong winds. The stairs are narrow and dark, so are not ideal for the claustrophobic.

One of the most striking features of the tower is its asymmetrical shape; it's almost circular but has a curving 'tail', representative of either

> **Maiden Baku**
> There's a great view of the Maiden's Tower, the Old City and the Caspian Sea from the rooftop restaurant of the nearby Sultan's Inn (p.202), while at the tower's base are some interesting carved stones, figures and excavations of a medieval bazaar.

one half of the yin-yang symbol or the Zoroastrian religious symbol for fire, some say. The myths surrounding the origin of the tower are as fascinating as the structure itself. The most romantic is that a young woman ordered the tower to be built so she could delay an unwanted marriage. Once completed, she jumped from the top into the sea (which in ancient times lapped its walls). Other theories on the building's name relate to it potentially being used to hide women during attacks on the city, or that it may be a reference to the defences never being overcome during battle.

Open from 10:00 to 18:00 every day except Monday.
Map 2 E6 **Metro** Icheri Sheher

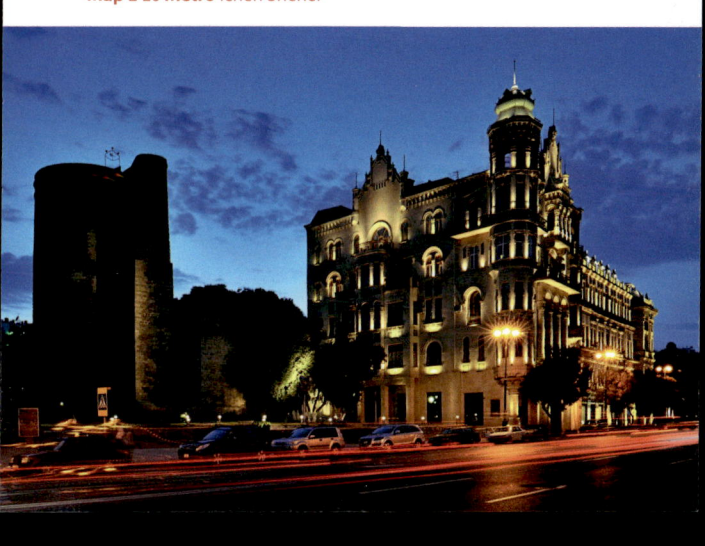

Exploring

Downtown Baku

Exploring

Downtown is best explored on foot, with its collection of parks and squares, theatres and museums, and interesting shops, cafes, restaurants and bars.

The Downtown area of Baku, loosely defined, covers much of the lower-central area of town; stretching east from Old City to the Landmark Building, and north of the Boulevard for 10 or so blocks, Baku's streets criss-cross in a grid-like layout. One of the main areas of public congregation, just outside the Old City walls, is Fountain Square. Re-opened in 2010 following a facelift, the square is a popular local hangout, particularly on weekends and public holidays. People come to the square to stroll about or simply to hang out, and the cascading water from the fountain makes it a soothing spot in quieter moments. It's typically at its busiest around 21:00, which is dinnertime for most Azeris.

Many of the museums are at this end of town, including the Literature and History museums (p.88), while both Nizami Street and Istiglaliyyat Street provide great places to shop for fashion (see Shopping, p.130).

Other small streets radiate out from the square too, and are home to all kinds of international restaurants, bars and clubs (see Going Out, p.154), as well as the famous MUM department store (p.146).

Further east, towards the Landmark Hotel (p.61), you'll come across something of interest on almost every block,

Heydar Aliyev Palace

including Khagani and Sahil Parks (p.100), both three blocks up from the Boulevard. The Opera and Ballet Theatre (p.93) is situated five blocks up from Park Bulvar mall, while Heydar Aliyev Palace (p.92) is another five blocks further in from that. Interesting shops, cafes and bars are dotted around this entire area, and again, the best way to explore is to simply take to the streets on foot.

Exploring

Around The City

Exploring the wider city affords great insights into Baku, as well as some great views and beaches.

To the south-west of the Old City is the Philharmonic Hall (p.94), and then a steep hill, which can be ascended using the funicular railway (p.55). The area at the top is known as Badamdar, and there are excellent views back across the bay. You'll also find Martyrs' Alley (p.98), a moving memorial park to Baku's fallen. The Botanical Gardens are up here too, as is a gigantic TV transmitter, which can be seen from around the city and is brightly lit at night.

The Hyatt area of town, as it is known locally, lies to the north of the city centre, and is home to both Hyatt hotels (p.61), a number of restaurants, and high-rise apartments and offices. To the north-east of the city centre is an area known as Ganjlik, which is where you'll find the Tofik Bahramov football stadium (p.126), the President's Palace, and an area of plush addresses known as Millionaire's Mile, all accessible from Ganjlik Metro station.

The area along the coast southwest of Baku Harbour is called Shikhov (or Shikh) Beach. Here you can find hotels like the Ramada (p.65) and the Crescent Beach (p.64), both of which offer access to the beach (and views of offshore oilrigs). The main bazaars are also nearby. Over on the other side of town, east of Javanshir Bridge, is the city's other main area, Khatai. The southernmost portion of this area, called

Baku's funicular railway

'Black City' (due to high concentrations of smoke and dirt), was where much of the oil was extracted at the turn of the century. Today, the worst of the industrial infrastructure is being replaced. The new Museum of Modern Art (p.86) is located here. The waterfront west of the Javanshir Bridge contains the city's port, and the area is currently under development, housing various post-modern high-rise buildings like the Port Baku and the new Marriott (p.58).

Exploring

Exploring

Art Galleries

There's a thriving art scene of small independent galleries and big national showcases in the capital.

Art is an important part of the cultural scene in Baku, and there are numerous private galleries displaying and selling works – particularly modern paintings – scattered throughout the city. Many of these smaller set-ups are clustered in and around the Old City. A decent picture or painting can make a great souvenir, and can be relatively inexpensive here. There are also two major galleries – the State Museum Of Art and The Museum Of Modern Art, both of which have extensive collections. Visit www.citylife.az to find the latest gallery exhibitions.

Absheron Gallery   012 492 2142
11 A Zeynally St, Old City
This gallery is a compact unit near the Shirvanshah's Palace in the Old City, hosting changing exhibitions and showcases. Entry is usually free. **Map** 2 E6 **Metro** Icheri Sheher

Ali Shamshir's Gallery   012 497 7136
84 Kichik Gala St, Old City
This gallery primarily displays the works of the eponymous Ali Shamshir. His compositions are dominated by poppies and women in red. The gallery is located in the Old City near the Shirvanshah's Palace. **Map** 2 E6 **Metro** Icheri Sheher

Art Gallery Vitru 012 492 2968
7 Husu Hajiyev St, Old City www.vitru-art.com
This very small gallery just off Fountain Square is a good place to head if you're looking for souvenir artwork. There are a range of watercolours from viewpoints around the Old City, as well as a series of amusing caricatures of Baku life.
Map 2 E5 **Metro** Icheri Sheher

The Azerbaijan State Museum Of Art 012 492 5789
9-11 Niyazi St, Old City
This museum is located just outside the Old City walls and, in the style of many official cultural institutions in Azerbaijan, is 'named after' a key figure from the relevant genre; in this case it's Rustam Mustafayev, an artist who created beautiful stage sets for the theatre. Housed in a turn-of-the-century oil boom mansion, the museum displays European, Russian and Azerbaijani art over three floors and largely features landscapes, portraits and sculptures. The exhibits on the third floor rotate, and the atmosphere is more formal than most other venues. Open every day except for Mondays, 10:00-18:00. Admission is AZN10. **Map** 2 D6 **Metro** Icheri Sheher

Centre For Contemporary Art 012 492 5906
15 Gulle St, Old City
This small gallery, located near Karavan Saray (p.184) in the Old City, displays and sells works by local, modern artists. It's open every day except for Mondays from 11:00 to 20:00 and admission is free.
Map 2 E6 **Metro** Icheri Sheher

www.liveworkexplore.com

Exploring

Art Galleries

Yusif Mirza's Studio 012 493 5285
4 Khagani St, Downtown
Yusif Mirza's studio is in a small, cave-like apartment accessed from an alleyway opposite the Russian Drama Theatre. Spread all over the studio, the work is inspired by the ancient cave drawings at Gobustan (p.106). **Map** 2 F5 **Metro** Sahil

Museum Of Modern Art 012 490 8404
5 Safarov Yusif St, Nr Javanshir Bridge, Khatai
The Museum of Modern Art is a great, spacious venue, located in the shadow of the Javanshir Bridge; you'll recognise it by the abstract sculptures outside. Displays include non-traditional Azeri art from the 1940s to the present. On the second floor, there's a room dedicated to works by western European masters including Picasso, Dali and Chagall; there's also an interesting display of local children's art. The museum has an extensive art book store and reading room, and there's a pleasant cafe too. Open daily, except Monday, from 11:00 to 21:00. Entry costs AZN5.
Map 2H3 **Metro** Khatai

Qiz Qalasi Gallery 012 492 7481
6 Gulle St, Old City www.qgallery.net
Qiz Qalasi is a private art gallery founded in 1999 by Salkhab Mamedov, an Azerbaijani professor of art, and his artist son Emin. Located in the shadow of Maiden's Tower, the gallery holds regular exhibitions of Azerbaijani and international artists. Open Monday to Friday from 10:00 to 19:00 (10:30-19:00 at weekends). **Map** 2 E6 **Metro** Icheri Sheher

Soviet era mural

Exploring

Art Galleries

www.liveworkexplore.com

Exploring

Museums

The country's traditions and cultural heritage are well represented in Baku's main museums.

There are a number of larger museums in Baku that offer visitors a good flavour of different aspects of Azeri culture. You can explore most of them satisfactorily in a couple of hours, and as they tend to be air-conditioned they make for a pleasant diversion during the sticky summer months. House museums, or residences where famous Azeri lived, are also common; the Bul-Bul Memorial Museum (15 Bul-Bul Ave, 012 493 5697) and the Rostropovich Museum (19 Rostropovich St, 012 492 0265) are good examples. This section lists the most popular museums; see also Art Galleries, p.84.

Carpet Museum, Theatre Museum & Museum Of Independence   012 493 6685
123 A Neftchilar Prospect, Downtown
www.icom.azeurotel.com

The Carpet Museum is one of Baku's iconic attractions, and showcases a proud national tradition. Located in the Museum Centre, a pseudo-Greek acropolis near the Boulevard, the building is an impressive example of Soviet-era architecture. Azeri carpets are known for their bold geometric designs and bright colours, but each type of carpet has unique characteristics. The old tradition of Azerbaijani carpet weaving is now included in UNESCO's intangible cultural heritage list.

Although the collection is impressive and extensive, only a fraction of the museum's 6,000 or so carpets are on display at any one time. You'll find both modern and antique types, as well as knotted and flat weave carpets from all regions. The museum collection includes 600 carpets from the Karabakh region, as well as traditional clothing, jewellery, shoes and copper goods like plates, jugs, mugs, and samovars. Open from 10:00 to 18:00 every day (except Mondays). Entry is AZN5.

You can also purchase tickets to the other two museums housed in the building. The State Museum Of Theatre displays programmes and costumes from Azeri theatre and the Museum Of Independence presents key historical events and people in Azerbaijan. **Map** 2 F5 **Metro** Sahil

History Museum
4 Z Taghiyev St
012 493 3648
www.icom.azeurotel.com

Housed in the Italianate former residence of Zeynalabdin Taghiyev, one of the richest oil barons of the 20th century, the History Museum is well worth a visit.

Exhibits on the lower floor include interesting information on archaeology and handicrafts, and help visitors build up a good picture of Azerbaijan's heritage. Upstairs, you can have a good look around Taghiyev's restored residence, which is even more opulent than the Shirvanshah's Palace (p.75). The residence features two ornate ballrooms, and a sitting room that is completely covered in tiny mirrors. Admission is AZN5 for adults, with an extra charge for a (recommended) two-hour guided tour. Open every day, except Sunday, from 11:00 to 16:30. **Map** 2 E5 **Metro** Sahil

Miniature Book Museum 012 492 9464
1 Gala St, Old City

The private Miniature Book Museum in the Old City opened in 2001 and is located near the Shirvanshah's Palace. Here you can find tiny books in a number of languages, with 3,700 fingernail size books displayed. Check out the smallest book in the world – a 3.5 millimetre by 3.5 millimetre book made in Japan – using tweezers and a magnifying glass. Admission is free but donations are accepted. It's open from 10:00 to 17:00, except on Mondays and Thursdays.
Map 2 E6 **Metro** Icheri Sheher

Nizami Museum Of Azerbaijan Literature 012 492 1069
53 Istiglaliyyat St, Old City

Nizami Ganjavi (1141-1209), after whom this museum is named, was one of the great romantic poets of Azeri literature, and the museum was originally devoted to his works, but has grown to cover other writers and now displays the development of Azerbaijani literature from ancient times to the present day.

Opposite the Old City's Double Gate, the exterior of the building is distinctive, with six archways showcasing statues of great Azerbaijani writers against a blue mosaic background – making them some of the most photographed in Baku. Open every day (except Sundays) from 11:00 to 17:00, entry costs AZN10 with another AZN10 for an English-speaking guide. **Map** 2 E5 **Metro** Icheri Sheher

Exploring

Museums

www.liveworkexplore.com 91

Exploring

Theatres & Entertainment Venues

With international performers as well as local shows, there is entertainment for all tastes in Baku.

Azerbaijan State Puppet Theatre
012 492 6435
36 Neftchiler Ave, Downtown   www.kuklateatri.com

This venue stages elaborate shows in Russian and Azeri, with ornate puppets as the stars of the show. The theatre building, which is very grand and shares some architectural similarities with the Philharmonic Hall, was built in 1910. Recent performances include Hans Christian Andersen's Thumbelina, but some productions are for adults only.

Map 2 E6 **Metro** Icheri Sheher

Heydar Aliyev Palace
012 498 8477
35 Bul-Bul St, Downtown

Baku's largest and most exclusive shows are staged at the Heydar Aliyev Palace, located next to Heydar Aliyev Park (the one with the gigantic Heydar Aliyev statue). Formerly known as Republic Palace or Lenin Palace, today it's the main venue for large rock concerts and state occasions, such as

> **Top Tickets**
> You can buy tickets for all of the key performance venues just off Fountain Square in the kiosk across from the Mozart Cafe (p.176).

presidential inaugurations, with seating for over 1,800 people. Tickets to shows are considerably more expensive than for other venues, typically costing anything between AZN20 and AZN150. **Map** 2 F4 **Metro** 28th of May

Musical Comedy Theatre   012 498 4917
8 Neftchiler Ave, Kubinka

Productions at this theatre, also known as Azerbaijan State Theatre of Musical Comedy, are usually less lavish than those at the Opera and Ballet Theatre. The building itself is not as grandly ornate either, and the facilities are on the basic side – but tickets are inexpensive (around AZN5) and recent performances have included Little Red Riding Hood and the operetta, Bayadera. Tickets can be purchased at the box office, or at the central ticket sales building near Fountain Square.
Map 2 E5 **Metro** Sahil

Opera & Ballet Theatre   012 93 3449
95 Nizami St, Downtown

Also known as the Azerbaijan State Academic Theatre of Opera and Ballet, this ornate building was renovated in

> **Azeri Opera**
> The Muslim world's first opera, Leyli and Majnun, written by Uzeyir Hajibeyov and based on the poetry of Nizami Ganjavi, was staged in Azerbaijan in 1908. Azeri opera tends to integrate aspects of traditional Azerbaijani music with classical western music. You can listen to samples in the music archive at www.azer.com.

1988, following a fire to the original. The early 20th century art nouveau facade has been retained and the interior also conveys turn-of-the-century grandeur, featuring sculpted figures and elaborate chandeliers. The productions held here are large-scale, with elaborate sets and costumes and high quality performance. Azerbaijani theatre etiquette is a little more relaxed than in the west, so don't be surprised if people talk or take photographs during the show. Ticket prices are comparatively inexpensive, usually between AZN11 and AZN16, and are available at the box office.

Map 2 F4 **Metro** Sahil or 28 May

> **Russian & Azeri Theatre**
> There are a couple of other options for live stage entertainment – the Azerbaijan State Russian Drama Theatre on Khagani Street, a few blocks from Fountain Square (012 493 0063, www.rusdrama-az.com) and Azerbaijan State Pantomime Theatre on Azadlig Avenue, near the American Embassy (012 441 4756). All performances are staged in Russian and Azeri (respectively) and are great ways to get an insight into the region's culture.

Azerbaijan State Philharmonia   012 497 2905
2 Istiglaliyyat St, Downtown

The Philharmonic Hall, or Azerbaijan State Philharmonia, is officially named after Muslim Magomayev, who composed

the classic Azeri operas Shah Ismayil in 1917 and Nargiz in 1935. The building is a stunning lemon and white coloured Italian Renaissance-styled construction, and re-opened in 2004 after a lengthy restoration process. Chamber and symphony concerts are regularly staged here, and tickets usually cost between AZN5 to AZN15. The venue has an impressive record of attracting high quality, international artists. Over the years luminaries of the musical world such as piano soloists Aleksandr Gindin (Russia), Sergey Kudryakov (Russia), and Jeroen van Veen (Holland) have performed here.
Map 2 D6 **Metro** Icheri Sheher

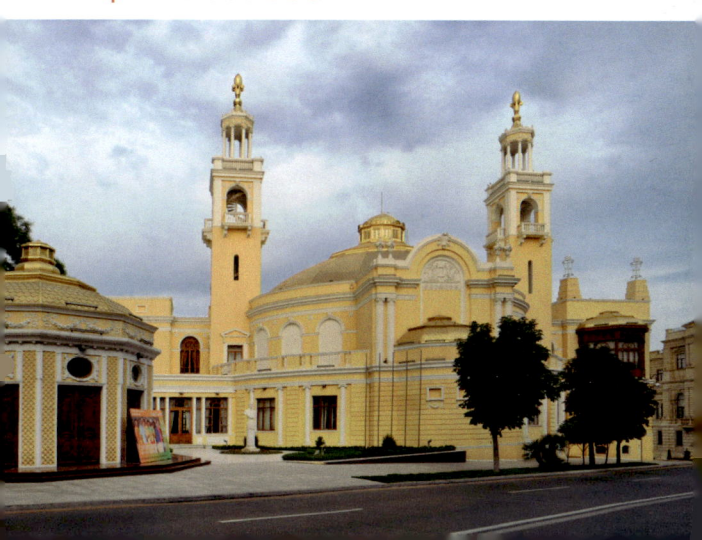

Exploring

Parks, Beaches & Attractions

The good people of Baku enjoy promenading, picnicking and playing in the city's many outdoor public spaces.

Parks

Baku has numerous small parks scattered throughout the city, providing great places to sit and play outside, and welcome shade in the heat of the summer. Green spaces are rare in this desert climate, and because of this, it's considered rude to walk on the grass or disturb the natural vegetation. With their dramatic and often colourful lights, the main parks come alive at night and are busy with Bakuvians taking in the sights and meeting friends and neighbours. The Boulevard, officially classed as a national park, is perhaps the most popular of all the city's parks.

Botanical Gardens
012 438 1172
40 Badamdar Highway, Badamdar   www.aznabatat.com

Founded in 1934, the Botanical Gardens contains a collection of local and exotic trees, bushes, and plants within its 45.7 hectares out in Badamdar. Although it's not a world-class garden, nor centrally located, it is a nice spot to stroll through the greenery, have a picnic, cycle, or go for a jog. Unlike the other parks, it is enclosed and entrance requires a ticket (AZN1 for adults, AZN0.5 for children).
Map 2 B7

Heydar Aliyev Park
Fizuli St Downtown

This park provides a backdrop for the Heydar Aliyev Palace Concert Hall and the Heydar Aliyev statue. The park has gleaming pink granite walkways, fountains in the shape of stars, and decent toilet facilities. There are a few trees, grassy patches and benches. The park is the venue for the annual Flower Festival in May, when some 1.5 million flowers are arranged to commemorate the birthday of the late President.
Map 2 F4 **Metro** 28 May

Huseyn Javid Park
Yasamal

This park, named after a prominent Azeri poet and playwright of the early 20th century, contains a cafe, benches and pine trees, but the main attraction for kids is the bouncy castle that operates during good weather (AZN1 for about 15 minutes). Attractions for adults include the dark and very dramatic statue of Huseyn Javid in the middle of a swirl of leaves, and an ornate fountain. **Map** 2 C4 **Metro** Elmlar Akademiyasi

---

Fun-set Boulevard

For some outdoor amusements, head to the Boulevard, where you'll find two beautiful European carousels just outside Park Bulvar mall. There is also a Ferris wheel and bumper cars. Each ride costs AZN2. Inside Park Bulvar is the Happy Land arcade, which keeps the young ones happy with games, bumper cars and bowling. Be aware, Azeris don't take kindly to being crashed into on the dodgems.
www.parkbulvar.az

Khagani Park
Khagani St, Downtown

The main attraction of this city park, formerly Molokan Garden, is the playground, which features a tall climbing frame, several slides and rock-climbing walls. There's also an attractive fountain with sleek sculptures, tall shady trees, elaborate birdhouses, plenty of flowers and rows of wooden benches making for a pleasant place to spend some time, and a busy spot at the weekend.
Map 2 E5 **Metro** Sahil

Martyrs' Alley
Sabayil

Martyrs' Alley, on the hillside leading to Badamdar, looking back over the city, was built in 1991 as a monument to those killed in the Soviet Army massacre in 1990 (see p.9). It has since become a cemetery for other war heroes. Give yourself an hour or more to fully explore the area.

A maze of walkways and steps leads to the eastern edge of the park from where you can view Downtown and the harbour, or take the funicular railway down the hill (p.55). If you continue south on foot you'll pass terraces of graves, which is one of the capital's most sacred (and haunting) places to linger. At the end of the rows of graves is a lookout point with a spectacular view and a teashop. Nearby there's a tall, open, sand-coloured monument with an eternal flame burning in memory of unnamed martyrs.
Map 2 D7 **Metro** Icheri Sheher

Exploring

Parks, Beaches & Attractions

Sahil Park
Downtown

Sahil (meaning 'shore' in Azeri) Park, a few blocks up from the Boulevard and Park Bulvar mall, extends for about one block and features grassy areas, a fountain, benches and palm trees, but there's not much for children to do. Rather, it's a place for adults to meet and enjoy the nearby cafes and restaurants, museums and library, as well as the Opera and Ballet Theatre (p.164). **Map** 2 F5 **Metro** Sahil

Zorge Park
Nasimi

At the northern edge of the city centre, this strip of parkland extends a block north of and parallel to Bakikhanov Street. The main area has grass, benches, pigeons, white-bottomed olive trees, a cafe and table tennis tables, with small rides and cars for children to drive. At its westernmost point, a dramatic statue peers out. The entire sculpture consists of one long black strip with only two large, stern eyes; it aptly commemorates the Azerbaijani secret service agent, Richard Zorge, who was killed by the Japanese during World War II. Away from the impressive, if slightly sinister monument, there's a children's play area, Koala Park, which features a number of small rides and attractions for the youngsters. **Map** 2 E2 **Metro** Ganjlik

Beaches & Attractions
There are a few beaches and waterparks providing summer fun in Baku. The Shikhov beach resorts are on the southern

end of Baku, near Badamdar about 10 kilometres from the Old City. They all offer the same type of coarse, yellow sand and the same view of the sea and distant offshore oilrigs. As with most places in Baku, access and costs can vary. See Beach Hotels, p.64, for details. Just beware that, while it may be tempting to feel the sand between your toes on the beach, it's not recommended that you wade or swim in the water in the south of the city because of health risks posed by the heavy water pollution. The beach resorts do all compensate by having extensive leisure facilities, including indoor and outdoor pools, sports halls, even an ice rink; and are also popular for its bars.

Exploring

Tours & Sightseeing

Using the services of a tour company can make getting to the more remote corners of the country a little easier.

If you want to take a guided tour of some of Baku and Absheron's main sights, or would like to have the hassles taken out of exploring the country, there are a number of tour companies that can arrange excursions around the capital and beyond, either to a set programme or on a tailor-made itinerary. Many also offer other services such as visa and arrival assistance, and also double up as international travel agencies. On the whole, tours tend to be fairly expensive, so it pays to shop around, always negotiate to get the best deal, and make sure you know exactly what is covered.

Tours & Sightseeing

Baki Tur	012 493 9630	www.bakitur.com
Caspian Travel	012 498 2508	www.caspiantravel.com
Dervish Travel	012 493 2919	www.dervishtravel.az
Elite Travel	012 449 9020	www.elite-travel.az
Improtex Travel	012 498 9239	www.improtex-travel.com
Khazar Travel	012 449 4361	www.khazar.travel
Millennium Tour	012 598 4818	www.millenniumtour.az
Pasha Travel	012 497 1090	www.pashatravel.az
Royal Travel	012 496 7966	www.royaltravel.az
Spektr Travel	012 493 6426	www.spektr.az

Baku's old city wall

Exploring

Tours & Sightseeing

www.liveworkexplore.com

103

Further Out

If you have the time, and the adventurous inclination, there is a fascinatingly diverse landscape to explore outside of the capital.

If you're in the country for an extended period of time, there is a lot for the adventurous to explore beyond the capital city itself. From the dramatic mountain scenery of the Greater Caucasus range in the north, down to the central plains and the sub-tropical south, the scope and variety of landscape in Azerbaijan is staggering.

Depending on your patience and stamina, you can get to almost any far-flung nook of Azerbaijan, whether you're interested in nature hikes through mountains and forests, or getting an up close insight into village life. And if you've only got a day or two to spare, there are some interesting sites just outside Baku on the Absheron Peninsula.

You can take organised or tailored trips from Baku with dedicated tour operators (p.102), or alternatively if you can secure a driver and/or car, you can head off independently. The options are many, but remember that you'll get the most out of your travels if you're willing to be flexible and make plans on the fly. It really is a place where it pays to follow your nose, take recommendations and get to know the locals. Speed and service may be frustrating at times, but think of travelling here as an adventure rather than a holiday, and you'll find it rewarding.

Absheron Peninsula

The Absheron Peninsula is the spit of land jutting out into the Caspian Sea, in the middle of which sits Baku. When you drive around this dusty industrialised land, you'll encounter pylons, oil derricks by the dozen and blotchy pools of oily waste that seem to stretch to the horizon. Yet nestled among these eyesores are features as old as the civilisation that first took hold here. A few miles north of Baku is Yanar Dagh, the burning mountain (around AZN25 for a round trip in a taxi). It's this type of feature that inspired Azerbaijan's ancient name, which roughly translates to 'The Land of Fire', and, as you approach, the view of the wall of flame leaping from the hillside is truly bizarre. You can stop here and have tea while enjoying the fire, which was supposedly lit from gas seeping out of the ground in the 1950s.

To the east on the peninsula is the Ateshgah fire temple; once the site of ancient Zoroastrian fire-worshippers, today it's home to a temple built by Indian traders. The flames around the temple's edges were once fed by a gas pocket below, but the gas is now piped in and only

> **Beach Resorts Of Absheron**
> While bathing on the shores of the Caspian is not comparable to basking on Caribbean sands or swimming in the Med, there are a number of beach resorts dotted around the Absheron Peninsula for a Baku style seaside escape. See Beach Resorts, p.64, for more details.

Exploring — Further Out

infrequently lights up the shrine. You can take a short train ride here from Baku or take the number 84 *marshrutka* from the Nariman Narimanov metro station.

To discover the truly ancient side of Absheron, head 60 kilometres south from Baku to Gobustan, the site of ancient carvings dating back to the Stone Age. The petroglyphs are carved into rock faces of cave dwellings, and the number of individual etchings is thought to be in the thousands, making it a designated UNESCO World Heritage Site. There is an AZN3 entry fee and an extra AZN2 for cameras, a well-spoken guide will take you around the site and through the small museum. For information, call the park service (012 544 4208).

Further south from Gobustan, towards the town of Alat, is an area of bizarre gurgling mud volcanoes. It's a little off the main track, but it's worth the effort. You can dip your hands in, but be careful – a wrong step could have you sliding down into the pits for an unexpected mud bath. You can also wander off to spot small oil pits of pure black gold. Getting there from Baku by taxi costs about AZN40 for a half-day round trip, or you can take a *marshrutka* or bus from Baku bus station to Gobustan town or Alat junction and hop in a taxi (AZN20) for the rest of the way.

Northern Azerbaijan

The north of the country is home to the breathtaking Greater Caucasus range – and with isolated villages, winding mountain roads and lush valleys, as well as a strip of coastal resorts, this area is well worth the two-hour drive from Baku. The region offers opportunities to explore a fascinating

The burning mountain of Yanar Dagh

Exploring

Further Out

www.liveworkexplore.com 107

history, ancient culture, and a beautiful natural environment set among rugged mountain ranges.

Just outside Baku the landscape becomes a dry, dusty flatland, hugged on one side by the Caspian Sea and on the other by the gently rising peaks of the Caucasus. Less than halfway to the northern region is the distinctive Five Finger Mountain towering over roadside rest stops. This solid rock outcropping looks like a hand reaching towards the sky above the highway.

Further north takes you into the heart of the Greater Caucasus range, home to the highest peaks in Azerbaijan. This cool, verdant region is also the country's orchard, and trucks loaded with apples and pears can be seen during the autumn. And when the cold winter sets in, this is one of the first regions of Azerbaijan to get a thick blanket of snow. The main towns of this region, Guba and Khachmaz, are spread out on relatively flat terrain, while there are numerous picturesque mountaintop towns overlooking winding roads and river valleys.

To the east, the Khachmaz region sprawls along the flatter plains of the Caspian coast and features Nabran, a beach town, popular with Bakuvians for its collection of large resorts nestled in the forest that stretches along the country's northern coastline.

The North-West

To travel into the north-western passage of Azerbaijan is to embark on an adventure through one of the most beautiful regions of the Caucasus. Home of the 18th century Sheki

Khanate, the region is speckled with aged fortresses and features an exquisitely restored khan summer palace.

Rolling north towards Georgia are the plump, grass-covered foothills of this cool, temperate zone. In spring, summer and autumn, the northwest region is a green, lush wilderness, then the winter snows come and transform the vista completely. As you explore the natural beauty of this Caucasus mountain stretch, you can indulge your senses in the flavours of regional foods and the bounty of produce unique to the region. Main towns include Sheki and Zagatala, but the real gems of the region are the mountain villages and scenery.

Also of interest is the region of Gakh, on the border with Georgia, famous throughout Azerbaijan as being home to some of the country's finest natural springs. The mineral waters in the region, particularly in and around the high-mountain village of Ilisu, are said to be medicinal, and there are a number of springs featuring bathing huts for people who want to 'take the waters'.

Western Azerbaijan

A journey from Baku through western Azerbaijan offers a real insight into this small country's conflicted history. While Baku is full of historical monuments and the centre of much of Azerbaijan's Soviet story, the western territories offer a glimpse into a very different past, set within the region's long, green plains and mountain ridges.

The west is home to the cities of Ganja and Mingachevir, the second and fourth-largest cities in Azerbaijan respectively. Ganja is a modern city that sprawls out along the Ganja River, but its history is flavoured by Russian and Persian empires, Khanates, Mongol rule, and Arab influences, and has also served as a cultural centre of the Caucasus and is known for its poets, composers, writers and artists. Mingachevir, by contrast, is a young city, founded in the late 1940s when a hydroelectric power station was built (with a large input from German POWs).

Both Ganja and Mingachevir are good stopping off points to explore the wider region where the highlights include Lake Goygol and its mountain passes, considered among Azerbaijan's most beautiful natural treasures. There are other activities geared up to visitors too, including wine tours of the region's vineyards (Goygol Wine Mill, www.vinagro.az), and the chance to take an 'oil bath' in the Goranboy region, which despite sounding distinctly unusual, is supposed to have skin-cleansing properties (Naftalan Sanatorium; www.naftalan-tour.com).

Southern Azerbaijan

The landscape of southern Azerbaijan is in stark contrast to the dusty desert stretches of the Absheron Peninsula. The road south from Baku, down towards the towns of Lankaran, Lerik and Astara, on the border with Iran, passes through parts of Azerbaijan known for an array of produce, religiosity, beautiful mountain views and local vacation spots.

The gently sloping Talysh Mountains that straddle the international border are the main geographical feature of this semi-subtropical region. Often shrouded in a light mist, these

The rural idyll of north western Azerbaijan

Exploring | Further Out

mountains, named after the region's Talysh people, have a quiet, mystical demeanour.

There are a number of national parks in the south too, including Shirvan National Park, Hirkan National Park, Gizilagach Reserve and Khanbolan Reserve. These constitute the majority of protected areas in southern Azerbaijan, and feature a multitude of flora and fauna that many Azerbaijanis are proud of, while throughout the area are numerous places featureing hot water springs that bubble up from beneath the mountains. Both Masalli and Lankaran have baths you can enjoy for just a few manat. One other notable feature of the south is the legendary longevity of the people of Lerik, who are said to live well into their hundreds thanks to their healthy mountain lifestyle.

Nakhchivan

Some Azerbaijanis say that Nakhchivan, the autonomous exclave to the south-west, on the other side of Armenia, is where you can find the original, authentic Azerbaijani language and culture. Nakhchivan translates as 'Colony of Noah' – the Noah of Old Testament fame.

Separated from the 'motherland', it's a small but characterful territory on the slopes of the Minor Caucasus mountains, and a visit here provides an altogether different experience. The original home of Heydar Aliyev and his family, along with much of the high leadership in government, Nakhchivan is governed separately, and this reflects in the way the republic feels and is laid out and run.

Nakhchivan city is small but interesting, and there are some spectacular mountain views to be had from the surrounding areas, including Ilan Dagh, 20km east of the city. It is said to be the peak that Noah's biblical ark skidded across before beaching on Mount Ararat, leaving a remarkable cleft in the rock.

Travel to Nakhchivan is only really possible by plane (unless you're willing to brave the bus ride through Iran and Julfa). Azal flies to Nakhchivan five or so times daily and one way flights cost in the region of $100 (www.azal.az). Entry into Nakhchivan requires no special pass or visa, although it's always best to check the latest visa regulations before starting out.

Nagorno Karabakh

One area of Azerbaijan that you cannot currently visit is Nagorno Karabakh. The region is currently occupied by Armenia and administrated by an internationally unrecognised government known as the 'Nagorno Karabakh Republic'.

The Azerbaijani position is unwaveringly firm: their country is the victim of a grave wrong-doing, their land has been stolen and unlawfully occupied, and Armenia is the undeniable aggressor. Getting to Nagorno Karabakh today is impossible from anywhere in Azerbaijan. If you enter from Armenia, you are likely to be prevented from subsequently entering Azerbaijan. Attempting to travel to Nagorno Karabakh is not recommended.

Spas & Sports

Active Baku	**116**
Spas & Fitness	**118**
Sports & Activities	**122**
Spectator Sports	**126**

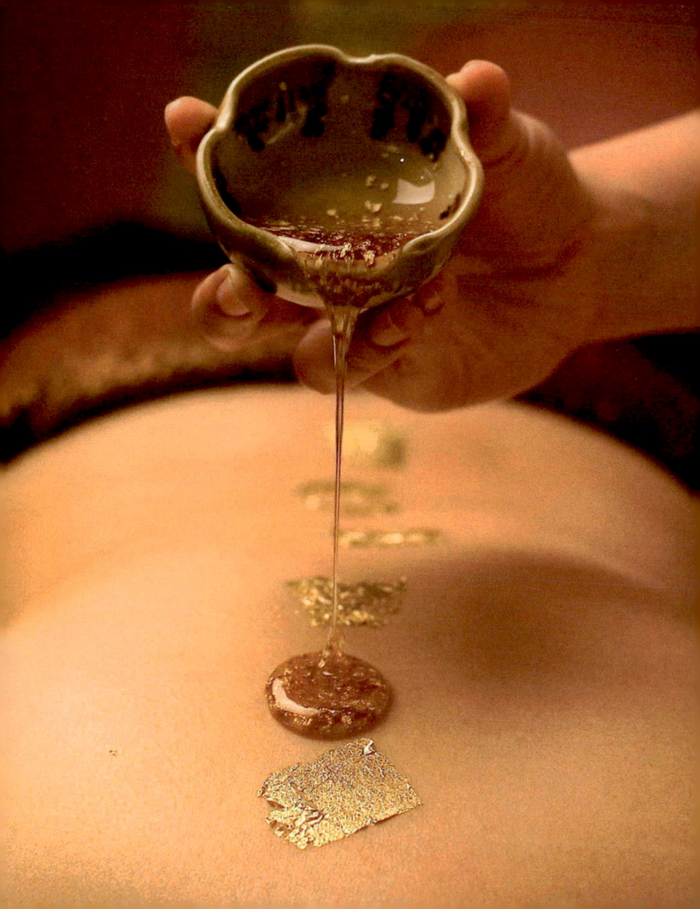

Sports & Spas

Active Baku

Those looking for a touch of pampering on their Baku break have a decent range of spas to enjoy and there are plenty of options for the more active.

There is a good selection of spas, gyms and beach clubs, particularly in the larger hotels and often for a reasonable price when compared to some of the world's more luxurious locations. More leisure facilities are expected with the imminent arrival of a raft of new five-star hotels (see p.58).

If you're looking for something more traditional, check out one of the city's older hamams (see p.119). Try the historic Taze Bey Hamam (012 492 64 40, www.tazebey.az), which was built in 1886 and was recently renovated. Treatments here include sauna rooms, plunge pools, birch treatments, massages, and even shoe cleaning. Like many establishments this one admits men only, but the Hamam Mehellesi, near the Old City metro, is open for women on Mondays and Fridays.

While Baku may not be considered a prime 'adventure playground' destination, it does have some good sporting options if you know where to look; the mountainous terrain of the country's interior offers some decent, if not easily accessible, mountain biking and hiking, and there's even some skiing to be had if you are determined enough.

Attending an Azeri football match is definitely a cultural experience worth having too, even if you may not have heard of some of the country's main teams.

Relax and unwind in one of Baku's hotel spas

Sports & Spas

Spas & Fitness

Travelling can take it out of you, so take advantage of Baku's growing spa options to revitalise yourself.

Health spas are popular in Baku, and saunas, in particular, have a long local heritage, with both men and women enjoying the benefits of relaxing in the hot steam. Over the past few years, a crop of new, modern spas have opened offering massages and body treatments. Almost all fitness centres also offer massages, generally at a reasonable price. The average rate for an hour-long massage is around AZN40.

Aqua Park
012 447 0303
59 Rashid Behbudov St, Nasimi
www.afhotel.az
Facilities include a fitness club, lap pool, saunas and massage. You can also opt to take one of several classes, including swimming, Pilates and aikido. Don't forget your swimming cap – entry into the pool without it is forbidden.
Metro 28th of May

Aqua Sport
012 495 2871
26 Abilov St Kubinka
Although the facilities are a little run down, there is a nice sauna and you can get very inexpensive massages here (from just AZN16). In addition to the 25m pool, Aqua Sport offers a small fitness centre. It also runs women-only sessions on Tuesday, Thursday and Saturday from 11:00 to 19:00.
Metro Nizami

Aura Wellness Centre 012 496 8000
Excelsior Hotel Baku Montin www.excelsiorhotelbaku.az

The spa at the Excelsior, one of Baku's grander hotels (p.60), offers a long menu of massage services in a truly tranquil setting. The Swedish massages are a popular choice, or guests can opt for a more niche treatment such as a hot stone or sea salt massage, and the spa offers Reiki and aromatherapy too. It also features perhaps the most luxurious fitness centre in Baku; the modern and stylish gym offers great equipment, a jogging track, saunas, massage, indoor and outdoor pools, a sundeck, and a summer garden. **Metro** Narimanov

Baku Entertainment Center 012 490 2222
130-33 Fazayil Bayramov St, Nr Ramstore, Khatai www.bem.az

The Baku Entertainment Center (a leisure and shopping complex in the Khatai area of the capital) has a Turkish bath and Finnish sauna, with day passes costing AZN30.

Club Oasis 012 490 1234
Hyatt Regency Baku, Nasimi
www.baku.regency.hyatt.com

The high-class Hyatt has a team of half a dozen expert massage therapists and it is usually possible to get a booking on the day. You don't have to be a hotel guest to use the spa, and

Hamam: Full Steam
A hamam is a traditional form of steam bath experience. Bathers are said to gain health benefits by immersing themselves in hot steam rooms, followed by a plunge into cold water, and also undertaking a massage or body scrub.

Spas & Fitness

the facilities were upgraded in 2010. Open seven days a week, with a unique and full range of treatments available, the club also has indoor and outdoor pools, state-of-the-art fitness equipment, an aerobics studio, table tennis, billiards, and tennis and squash courts.

Club Olympus
012 490 7090
Grand Hotel Europe, Yasamal
www.grand-europe.com

The Club Olympus is an interesting and beautiful alternative to the Hyatt if you are staying in the area but not at one of the hotels. Facilities here include a fitness centre with gym, sauna, plunge pool and outdoor pool, while there are classes in step, Pilates, aerobics, karate, aikido and dance.

The Landmark Health Club
012 465 2000
90A Nizami Street,
Downtown/Nasimi
www.thelandmarkhotel.az

It's not hard to get in the relaxation zone in this new health club at the well-known hotel that lives up to its name. As well as treatments, there is a heated indoor pool, steam room and

---

> **New Hotels Means New Spas**
>
> Several top-end hotels are set to open in Baku in the next couple of years, which will significantly boost the luxury spa market. Look out for the health and fitness offerings from Hilton, JW Marriott, Four Seasons, Kempinski, Dedeman and Fairmont over the coming months.

sauna. After your massage, unwind and enjoy the Caspian views at the Landmark's Vitamin Bar, located on the Panorama Sun Terrace. **Metro** Jafar Jabbarli or 28th of May

Sabun Nga Spa   012 497 0800
Zardabi St, Nr Matbuat St Yasamal   www.sabunngaspa.com

As one of the few spas in Baku not affiliated with a hotel, this high-end Thai spa offers a unique experience. Guests can indulge in complete rejuvenation programmes for the mind, body and spirit with a variety of massage and relaxation techniques. In addition, a sumptuous Thai meal can be served in private dining rooms. It's a tranquil oasis in the centre of bustling Baku, perfect for pampering.

Sports & Activities

Sports & Spas

Take it easy on one of the Caspian beaches near Baku, or get active and head out for an adventure into the spectacular Azeri back country.

Beach Clubs & Watersports

There are a number of Caspian coastline beaches within reasonable proximity of Baku, and some of the main hotels at the most popular spots have beach clubs that offer health, fitness and relaxation facilities, as well as some watersport options. Many operate long-term membership schemes for Baku residents, but you can also usually get day passes too if you fancy a beach break while in Baku – call ahead to check the latest details. Most beaches are within an hour's drive of the city, and your hotel should be able to help arrange transport.

Amburan Beach Club
012 453 8685
Bilga District, Nr Mardakan
Bilga Settlement
www.amburan.com

This club, on the northern shore of the Absheron Peninsula, has a good range of organised activities throughout the day, including beach volleyball, water aerobics, beach football and a huge bouncy castle for kids. There is a clean beach with sunbeds and umbrellas, cabanas and a beach bar. The pool has loungers with comfortable cushions, shaded areas and a snack bar, and there's a restaurant and nightclub. Entry is AZN18 per adult and AZN15 per child.

The Crescent Beach Hotel & Leisure Resort   012 497 4777
Salyan Highway, Shikhov Beach
Shikh Settlement   www.cbh.az

Just south of Baku, the Crescent Beach Hotel is long-established and boasts a good range of facilities and restaurants, in addition to swimming pools and a long stretch of beach where waterskiing, jetskiing, laser sailing and windsurfing are all on offer. Membership of the beach club here includes use of the leisure facilities, such as the fully equipped gymnasium, Jacuzzis, billiards room and squash and tennis courts. In the summer, it's home to an open-air disco which hosts international DJs. Day admission is available from around AZN20.

Khazar Golden Beach Hotel & Resort   012 554 0710
Sahil Beach Mardakan   www.khazarbeachhotel.com

This resort lies around 10km to the north of the airport, and while the facilities here are not quite up to the standards of Amburan, and there are fewer activities aimed at children, there is a good pool and a clean beach from where jetskis can be hired.

Ramada Hotel Health Club   012 491 7303
Ramada Baku, Salyan Highway,
Shikhov Beach   www.ramadabaku.com

Located on Shikov beach, next to the Crescent Beach Resort, the Ramada features a modern health club with excellent weights and cardio equipment, as well as indoor and outdoor swimming pools, steam room, Jacuzzi and massage. It also offers watersports options such as jet-skiing, and has a stretch of private beach.

Bowling

Ten-pin bowling is a popular pastime for Bakuvians, and there are quite a few bowling venues around the city where you can enjoy a game. The quality of facilities is very similar to that of most western countries, although the food available usually has more of an Azeri twist. Friday and Saturday evenings tend to be very busy and you may have to wait for a lane to open up. Games cost from AZN6 per person. You'll find lanes at Baku Entertainment Center on Fazayil Bayramov Street (www.bem.az) and Olympik Star (012 449 49 01) on Yusif Vazir Chaman Zaminli Street in Nasimi, but the newest offering is at the Park Bulvar mall (see p.152) on the Boulevard.

Golf Gap

If you like to play a round or two of golf while you're on your travels, you'll be out of luck in Baku. There are currently no proper 18 hole courses in Azerbaijan, although there are plans to build one as part of the $270 million Dream Island project in Bina, around 15km from the capital. The complex will also include a business centre and resort, but completion remains years rather than months away – so, for now, leave your clubs at home.

Mountain Biking

There are some good biking spots within reach of Baku, and also further afield in the country's mountainous regions. The potential for exploiting some great terrain is still very much untapped, but if you're the adventurous sort that can of course be advantageous. If you want to get the benefit of some good local knowledge, get in touch with the Baku Bicycle Club, a dedicated group of mountain biking enthusiasts run by expats (contact Sara McNeill at aurorablonde@gmail.com for more details). Highlights include McLeary's Ridge on the western edge of Baku, and a triple ridge that incorporates the dramatically named Buckworth's Vertical Suicide and Spaghetti Junction. The BBC also ventures further afield, tackling routes at places like Gobustan, Shamakhi, Guba, and the Talysh mountains.

Skiing in the Caucasus

Skiing has not yet been exploited as a leisure opportunity, but if you are determined to get on the slopes there could soon be an option. The mountainous areas of Azerbaijan enjoy a similar annual snowfall to the higher altitude Alps and there is a ski resort under construction near Gusar in the north. The Shahdag resort, in this area of outstanding natural beauty, is slated to be completed towards the end of 2011 and eager skiers can follow its progress on www.shahdag.az.

In the meantime, head for Georgia. It's just a short flight away, has two established resorts, Gudauri (www.gudauri.ge) and Bakuriani, and, as a bonus, you get to indulge in delicious Georgian cuisine.

Spectator Sports

Sports & Spas

Sports fans are in for a cultural treat in Baku where following national sports is a colourful and passionate affair.

Football is one of Azerbaijan's favourite sports and Azeri league clubs regularly compete in Europe's elite competitions (in the early stages at least). International games, which have seen the likes of Germany, England and Russia visit for European Championships and World Cup qualifiers over the past few years, are held at the Tofik Bakhramov National Stadium in Baku, near Ganjlik Metro station.

For English football fans, even if there's not a match on, the stadium is worth a visit. It is named after the Azeri (not Russian, as is commonly claimed) linesman whose controversial decision was responsible for the third English goal being allowed in the 1966 World Cup Final against West Germany, making him a national hero in England as well as in Azerbaijan. There's a statue of the man himself, flag aloft, in front of the ground.

Another name familiar to English football fans is that of Tony Adams; the ex-Arsenal and England captain was appointed in 2010 as manager of Qabala (Gabala) FC, who play in the recently formed Azerbaijan Premier League, and was tasked with winning the national league with his team. If you're interested in keeping up with the Englishman, *AZ Mag* (www.az-magazine.com) has regular articles following Adams' progress. Several of the clubs in the league of 12

Ball sports, both ancient and modern, are popular in Azerbaijan

Spectator Sports

Sports & Spas

Spectator Sports

teams are based in Baku; FK Baku and Neftchi Baku both play in the Tofik Bakhramov stadium; MOIK Baku play in the MOIK stadium; and Inter Baku and AZAL both share the Shafa Stadium. Don't expect the highest technical standards of world football, but do expect an interesting cultural experience.

There are other professional sports that are popular too, including wrestling, which is considered to be Azerbaijan's national sport. See the country's official wrestling federation website, www.awf-az.org, for the latest information on upcoming contests which, again, make for a fascinating if unusual cultural insight. Gymnastics is also popular, as a result of Azerbaijan's Soviet past, and there is a federation for this sport that details spectator events (www.agf.az). And hockey, both men's and women's, is played to a decent level as well (see www.azhf.az for details). If you're keen to catch some of the action you should also check local listings to see what's on during your visit.

The Heydar Aliyev Sports and Exhibition Complex next to the Hyatt hotels (p.61) has staged some recent international events, including European and world championships in rhythmic gymnastics, wrestling and taekwondo. There are also plans to construct a huge new venue, to be named Baku Olympic Stadium, with a 60,000-plus capacity, at the northern edges of Baku. When it opens the venue will host all major sporting events, replacing the rather antiquated Tofik Bakhramov as the national stadium, and it is hoped it will aid Azerbaijan in future bids to host international sporting competitions.

Sports & Spas

Spectator Sports

Shopping

Buying In Baku	132
Where To Go For…	136
Areas To Shop	146
Markets & Bazaars	148
Shopping Malls & Department Stores	152

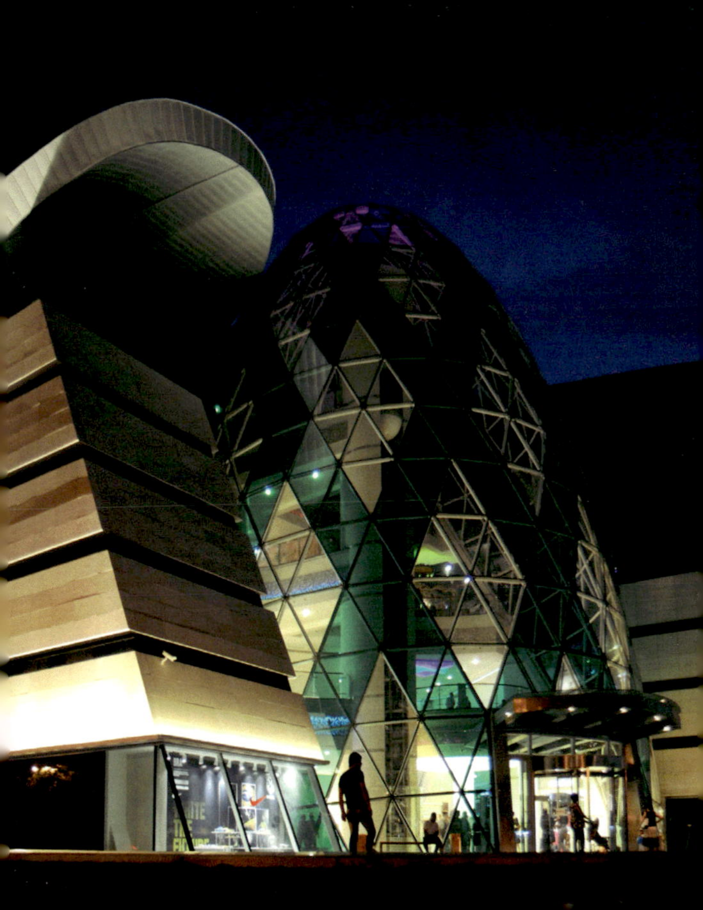

Buying In Baku

Baku's shopping options are growing and those with a keen eye for fashion and a nose for sniffing out hidden gems will have plenty to explore.

Baku may not fall into the same category as the likes of Paris, Dubai or New York when it comes to shopping possibilities, but there are definitely some good options whatever your budget. Over the past few years, more and more world-class outlets and brands have arrived in the city to cater for the nouveau-riche and expat communities. As a result, the upscale Boulevard is lined with the likes of Versace (www.versace.com), Christian Dior (012 437 6202) and Gucci (012 498 0055), while the new shopping mall, Park Bulvar (p.152), houses even more. Prices are markedly higher than in Europe or the US; expect to pay from 20% to 50% more. There are bargains to be had during annual sales, so you may get lucky.

For the earnest bargain hunters there are various markets and bazaars (p.148) where you'll find cheaper goods. Baku is a refreshing shopping destination as the selling culture is decidedly non-pushy. That said, if you are a fan of haggling, price reductions are possible for those who've mastered the art of negotiation (see Bargaining, p.134). Some of the most interesting shopping occurs in the small carpet, art and antique shops (p.138), mainly located in the Old City. You can spend hours sipping tea while getting to know the traders, most of whom speak English, meaning you can have a cultural as well as a haute couture experience when shopping.

Shopping

This chapter guides you through where to head for specific items such as carpets, clothes and collectibles, the shopping highlights of the different parts of town, and where to enjoy an Azeri bazaar experience.

Sizing

Figuring out your size isn't rocket science, it's just a bit of a pain. First, check the label – international sizes are often printed on them. If not, ask the sales people. They may be able to help you convert the printed size into one you understand. Otherwise, a UK size is always two higher than a US size (so a UK 10 is a US 6). To convert European sizes into US sizes, subtract 32 (so a European 38 is a US 6). To convert European sizes into UK sizes, a 38 is roughly a 10. As for shoes, a woman's UK 6 is a European 39, or a US 8.5, and a men's UK 10 is a European 44 or a US 10.5.

Bargaining

The practice of bargaining in Azerbaijan is alive and well. In many of the outdoor markets and bazaars, bargaining is expected; you may be surprised by how little 'give' the sellers have though. Offer a price that is 20-30% less than the asking price. The seller will almost always say no, then make a counter offer (or, at times, stick to his original price). You may only end up with a 5-10% discount, but it's better than nothing. In most boutiques and international stores, you're stuck with the sticker price – but don't be shy about asking for a discount. Occasionally, the seller will take off 10% if you simply ask.

Shipping

There are lots of options when it comes to shipping items out of the country. The least expensive method is through the Azerbaijani post office. This is a great choice for low-value items, when you're not in a hurry. For a small box, expect to pay around AZN2 to AZN3. If you prefer to use a private company, both DHL (012 493 4714, www.dhl.com) and UPS (012 493 3991, www.ups.com) ship to Europe and the US. Although you can't get next day delivery, your package should arrive in three to five days. You can call the company and they will pick the package up from your home and provide you with a receipt and tracking number. This isn't your best bet if you're sending heavy items as rates are quite expensive. If you're shipping certain cultural items, you'll need to obtain a certificate stating they are eligible for export. This applies to carpets, ethnic utensils, paintings, and pre-1960 musical instruments. Several companies, including Gosselin Caucasus & Central Asia (012 598 1920, http://gcca.gosselinwwm.com) and Interdean Ltd (012 447 4346, www.interdean.com) can help you navigate this process, as well as ship the items.

A Bottle Of Pinot...

Oenophiles may be interested in sampling a bottle of the region's famous Pinot Noir. Vineyards in Azerbaijan account for about 7% of the country's cultivated land, making it the main producers in the Caspian Sea region. Try specialist shops like Wine City (012 437 28 86, 76 Lermontov) or Lavinia (012 498 6489, 3/5 Rasul Rza St).

www.liveworkexplore.com

Shopping

Where To Go For...

Art

The art scene in Baku is a unique, sometimes quirky, one, but is fun to explore and you could find something quite novel for your collection. The best place to get acquainted with modern Azerbaijani art is the newly-opened Museum of Modern Art (p.86, 012 490 8404), which contains over 800 works from Azerbaijani painters and artists.

Qiz Qalasi Art Gallery (012 492 7481, 6 Gulle Street, www.QGallery.net), located in the shadow of the Maiden's Tower, is a beautiful gallery with a wide selection of contemporary Azerbaijani art, while Virtu Art Gallery (012 492 2968, www.vitru-art.com) is hidden on a side street near MUM (p.153). It shows a collection by local artists and is worth a visit for Sabir Chopuroghlu's work. His medium is, fittingly, crude oil – suitable given Azerbaijan's large reserves of the stuff. Another commercial art gallery, Yeni Gallery (012 598 4548, 6 Aziz Aliyev St, www.yenigallery.net), is located close to the seaside Boulevard. For Azerbaijani sculptures and handicrafts, check out Boyuk Gala 19 Art Gallery (012 492 0578) in the Old City, which shows and sells more traditional Azerbaijani artwork, or try Tatyana Agababayeva (012 566 2488, 9 Tehrnyayevski St, Montin) for batik work.

During the winter holiday season, various charity organisations hold art and craft bazaars, where local artists display and sell their work. Check the international newspapers for listings. Also be on the lookout for travelling exhibitions. The city hosts its International Art Festival (p.84) with exhibitions each year featuring both Azerbaijani and international artists (contact the Qiz Gallery for festival dates).

Carpets

Visiting Azerbaijan and not going carpet shopping is akin to taking a trip to Paris and not ticking off the Eiffel Tower. Azerbaijani carpet weaving made it on to Unesco's representative list of the Intangible Cultural Heritage of Humanity in November 2010, cementing the importance of this tradition in local and international cultural heritage. Carpets are intricately woven into the cultural history of Azerbaijan and even if you have no interest in purchasing, you should at least take a peek. The best place to start is the Carpet Museum (p.88) on Neftchilar Avenue. The museum is organised geographically and each room has a collection of carpets from the Azerbaijani regions.

Most of Baku's carpet shops are located in the Old City. You can spend an entire day going from shop to shop. At each location, the sellers will offer you tea and take out rugs for you to inspect. There is, of course, no obligation to buy. If you do find something you like be sure to negotiate. Don't be afraid of insulting someone with a low offer – the banter is all part of

Paintings By Numbers

Azerbaijan International Magazine **has created a fantastic website (www.azgallery.org) featuring local artists. You can browse selected works from several dozen artists and either contact them directly or with the help of the magazine staff if you don't speak Russian or Azeri. Some favourites include Yusif Mirza (012 493 5258) and Altai Sadigzade (012 439 7375).**

the game and the vendor will never sell at a loss. Many of the carpet shops also sell an assortment of new and antique goods such as samovars, scarves, tea sets and saddle bags.

Shops to look out for in the Old City include: Brothers' Carpet (13/6 Kichik Gala, 012 492 7166), run by three brothers; Flying Carpet Shop (10 Gulle St, 055 848 1310); Dargah Carpet Center (9 Rzayeva St, 050 305 8033), above the Mugam Restaurant; Kanan Huseynov's Carpet Shop (10 Gulle St, 050 647 3647), where the owner speaks very good English; Samir's Carpet & Antique Shop (Gala St, 051 862 1862); Seyed's Carpet Shop (63 Asef Zeynalli, 012 447 9363); and Togrul Carpet Shop (18/1 Boyuk Gala St, 055 712 0898).

Prices for carpets vary dramatically, depending on materials and age, but a budget of AZN400 should get you something special. However, if you're after a room-sized silk carpet expect to pay in excess of AZN3,000.

> **Shipping Your Carpet Home**
>
> Considered part of Azeri cultural heritage, antique carpets cannot be exported. In order to take your carpet home you need a certificate stating it is not an antique and is eligible for export. All sellers can arrange this for you, or get it yourself at the Carpets Exhibition Centre in the Old City, open Monday, Wednesday and Friday from 10:00 to 13:00. It costs AZN36 to get the certificate in a month, AZN42 in a week and AZN60 in an hour.

Traditional carpets

Where To Go For... **Shopping**

www.liveworkexplore.com 139

Fashion

With oil comes money and with money comes glitz. Take a stroll down Baku's main drag and you'll quickly see the transformation this once-Soviet backwater has made to a modern-day boomtown. The likes of Christian Dior, Bvlgari and Gucci boutiques bear witness to the economic revival.

If you have money burning a hole in your pocket, you'll have no trouble disposing of it in the many Baku high street shops or the posh new shopping mall, Park Bulvar (p.152). Fashionistas should head straight to Neftchilar Prospect, where the largest concentration of high-end boutiques is located. For most people though, it's just a great place to do some window-shopping.

You should have no problem getting your mitts on fashionable handbags and accessories in Baku, whether the real or the not-so-real varieties. Bottega Veneta (11 Rasul Rza St, 012 492 3399, www.bottegaveneta.com) specialises in beautiful, high-end leather handbags and accessories. Hong Kong (p.182) sells knock-off Louis Vuitton, Marc Jacobs, and Kate Spade bags, although prices can easily reach AZN100. For stylish but budget-conscious shoppers many of the mid-range accessories stores carry handbags, including Accessorize (Park Bulvar, 012 598 7144), Nine West (012 598 7137, www.ninewest.com), and Allure (4 Aziz Aliyev St, 012 598 5351, www.allurehandbag.com).

Bargain shoppers should be on the lookout for sales when stores, whose prices are normally severely marked-up compared to other international outlets, slash their prices. Away from the sales there are some better value stores. Local boutiques like Romantic (79 Nizami St, 012 493 3706) are great for casual dresses, starting at around AZN25. Adana (47 Istigaliyyet, 055 443 2000) is the best place to buy kids' and adults' T-shirts. It carries knock-off brand names in addition to old World Cup fare, starting at AZN5. If you're in the market for an Italian suit you have many options, from high-end names like Pal Zileri (83 Neftchilar Ave, 012 492 2249) and Ermenegildo Zegna (89 Neftchilar Prospect, 012 497 8923, www.zegna.com) to more affordable fare at Canali (8 Rasul Rza, 012 493 4306, www.canali.it) and Albatros (89 Neftchilar Prospect, 012 497 1197). For more casual wear, United Colors of Benetton (68 Bul-Bul Ave, 012 498 82 00, www.benetton.com) and RodiMood (42 Rashid Behbudov St, 012 498 91 08, www.rodimood.tr.gg) are good options for the guys.

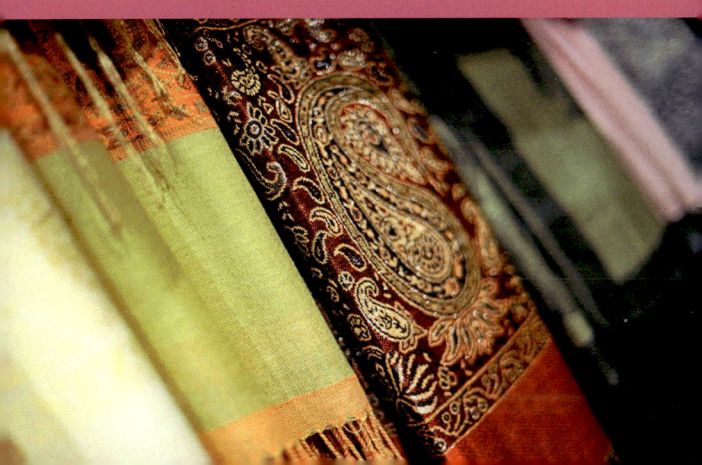

Shopping

Shopping

Where To Go For...

Shoe shopping has become increasingly fun in Baku as more international brands have moved in. Nine West recently opened in Park Bulvar, while more utilitarian styles can be found at Clark's (5 Uzeyir Hajibeyov St, 012 596 0309, www.clarks.co.uk) and Ecco (21 Jaffar Jabbarli St, 012 597 0604, www.ecco.com), near Molokan Gardens. There are several branches of Bata (91 Nizami St, 012 437 9554, www.bata.com), which is popular with expats and locals alike. Great deals can be found on footwear at the Airport Bazaar (p.149), which stocks everything from trainers to stilettos.

Music

Baku has a thriving music scene, including both classical, popular, rap and jazz (Baku was the jazz capital of the Soviet Union and to this day, many Azerbaijanis remain huge fans of the genre). You can find most international brands of instrument in Baku, as well as a fantastic selection of national instruments, of which there are many, and which make a great authentic souvenir for visitors. Melodiya (93 Azadliq Prospect,

Azeri Instruments

Azerbaijan has a fascinating variety of native musical instruments, including the stringed tar, a variation on the lute featured on the one manat note, percussion instruments such as the ghaval and the double-faced naghara, the accordion-like garmon, and the balaban, a reed instrument that looks similar to a recorder.

012 440 8596) has a good selection of traditional and modern instruments. Music Land (36 Khagani St, 012 498 0588) is a charming little store packed with instruments, where you'll find a great selection of local pieces, including kamanchas and tars; expect to pay about AZN250 for a kamancha. Royal (24 Nizami St, 012 418 7602, www.royal.az) is stocked with absolutely stunning antique Azerbaijani pieces, in addition to modern instruments; both high-end expensive items and more reasonably priced basic instruments are available. You can get some good recordings of Azeri music from stores such as ABC Audio-Video City, on Taghiyev Street near Fountain Square. Staff will be happy to point you in the right direction for Azeri jazz or for some examples of the traditional mugham form of folk music (see p.163).

Souvenirs

Souvenirs run the gamut in Baku, from tacky Maiden's Tower snow globes to tasteful (and expensive) samovars and tea sets. Two symbols that show up everywhere in Azerbaijan – the Buta (a decorative pattern style representing fire in Sanskrit) and the evil eye – are commonly found on souvenir items. Buta scarves are particularly popular and can be bought at carpet shops as well as the Airport Bazaar. Just keep your eyes open, so to speak, and you'll be sure to see an evil eye or two.

The highest concentration of souvenir stores and stands can be found in the Old City, where most carpet dealers (p.137) also sell old copper and bronze items, scarves and smaller trinkets and souvenirs. You can also find nice souvenir stands on the first floor of the Nargiz Plaza (p.153) that sell a wide array of small trinkets, while on the second floor of the Khagani Centre, near Fountain Square, the Iranian Shop & Carpet Gallery (012 498 4885) has a beautiful selection of filigree silver jewellery, wooden boxes and clothing imported from Iran. The Museum Centre (012 598 3731) also has a small gift shop on the first floor that features cards made by local artists. There's a great little photography shop in the Old City near the Swiss Embassy. No sign marks the entrance, but ASIM Photographer (11 Boyuk Gala, 050 319 0057) has some fantastic pieces of photography on sale, including classic black and white 'old men hanging out on street corner' scenes. Several framing shops sell spectacular reprints of turn-of-the-century oil boom photographs; these include The Frame Shop (21 Zarifa Aliyeva St, behind the Museum Centre, 012 598 2798).

For traditional central Asian items, check out the Art Boutique (10/12 Uzeyir Hajibeyov St, 012 498 0401), which has pottery, jewellery, scarves, vases and art. Suvenir Handmakers (20 Islam Saferli, 012 701 0144) is a very interesting shop near Fountain Square selling beautifully carved wooden pieces. A perfect souvenir for chocolate lovers can be picked up at either Caspian Crystal's Gastronomy (012 537 1599), which carries a sweet line of Baku themed chocolates, or Moskva Shirniyyat Evi (121 Lermontov St, 012 497 0783) which deals in Russian chocolate – in particular, the classic Alenka chocolate bars. Traditional local musical instruments make for an authentic souvenir (see p.143), and for pieces of art there is an eye-catching local scene (p.20).

There are many options for beautiful traditional mementos

Shopping

Areas To Shop

For ambiance and history, for alfresco meanderings, or for seriously stylish shopping spaces, there are areas of all ilks in Baku.

Azerbaijan Prospect

Leading north from the Old City, this street is home to at least half a dozen shops catering to kids, including Prenatal and Motherhood Maternity. At the south end is the Soviet-era department store, MUM (p.153), while further up you'll find a collection of textile and linen stores.

The Boulevard

The super rich shop along this strip. International luxury brands with over-the-top showrooms line Neftchilar. These boutiques not only carry stunning watches, jewellery and clothing, but are located in some beautiful spaces, with modern showrooms occupying turn-of-the century beaux-art style mansions. Boomtown Baku at its best.

Fountain Square

Just north of the Boulevard, you'll find a collection of small boutiques lining Fountain Square. The plaza is a fantastic place for a stroll and there are many great bistros and cafes where you can stop to relax and grab a bite to eat. Nargiz Plaza (p.153) sits at the north-east corner of the square and houses a nice mix of international and local brands.

Husein Javid Street

Located north of downtown near Baku State University, this stretch has a great mixture of shops, including Villeroy & Boch, Gallery Gifts & Flowers, and several clothing boutiques. When you need a break, swing by Baku Roasting Company (012 510 9876) for some of the best coffee in the city.

Istiglaliyyat Street

This major thoroughfare rings the north end of the Old City and is book-ended by the Presidential Administration to the west and Fountain Square to the east. You'll find a mix of international brands like Calvin Klein and Yves Rocher, along with local boutiques, and sights like the Philharmonic, Louvre-inspired Old City Metro, Baku City Hall and the stunning façade of the Nizami Museum of Literature.

Old City

If you're looking for carpets or art, the Old City is a great place to start. Most of the carpet vendors are located in clusters around the Maiden's Tower or the Double Gates. You won't find a better ambiance or sense of history anywhere else in town.

Nizami (Targova) Street

Leading east from Fountain Square is a lovely pedestrian strip, called alternatively Targova Street (the old Soviet name) or Nizami Street. There are several small shops along the newly renovated street, but the best time of the year to visit is December when vendors pitch up to offer a wide selection of holiday decorations and miniature Christmas trees.

Markets & Bazaars

For a great slice of local life, plus the chance to pick up something unusual, a visit to one of the city's small markets is highly recommended.

While Baku might not have the tourist-pleasing bazaars to match the likes of Istanbul or Tunis in terms of size or range, what it does offer is small but busy markets full of local character. Fresh fruit and vegetables are the main commodities that you'll find at the markets in Baku, and even if you're not looking to fill your suitcase with foodstuff it's a fascinating way to get an insight into day-to-day city life. Stall upon stall of apples, peaches, berries, lemons, onions, tomatoes, peppers, herbs and whatever else is in season await the adventurous shopper. Elderly village women sit outside the markets hawking homegrown produce and mysterious concoctions in old Coca-Cola bottles, and due to the nature of the product on offer you're unlikely to get the hassle you might encounter in the more commercial bazaars in other countries.

Of course, there's more than food at many of Baku's markets. You'll stumble across electronics, nuts and bolts, odds and ends like light bulbs, and much more. Unlike at some of the supermarkets, you won't find many vendors who speak English, making it a superb place to practise your Azeri or Russian. The markets are particularly busy on Sundays, so that's a good day to visit if you want a taste of local colour (but less so if you want a quiet shopping experience). You may also notice book sellers on the streets near the Landmark and opposite the Dom Soviet, displaying hundreds of second-hand volumes and dog-eared tomes that busy Baku workers often stop to leaf through. They are mainly non-English, but are worth a browse to see what you can uncover.

8 Kilometre Bazaar

Although it's a bit of a hike to get here, the 8 Kilometre Bazaar has, hands down, the cheapest produce in the city. Here you can pick up a bag of ripe, beautiful tomatoes for as little as AZN1. Although you can also find some clothing and other accessories here, you'll have to dig for that diamond in the rough. 51-55 Gara Garayev Prospect, between Khalglar Dostlughu and Gara Garayev metro stations.

New Airport Bazaar

Previously situated out near the airport but now relocated to just off the Salyan Highway in Garadagh, Sederek & Bina Bazaar (the new Airport Bazaar) is a well-known Baku institution for bargain hunters, but it's no tourist attraction. Situated on acres of land, housing hundreds of vendors and selling everything from teapots to car tyres at rock bottom prices, the market is so large that each vendor is given an address, using four points of reference: zone, building, korpus and store number. If curiosity gets the better of you, you can get there by bus (routes 137, 193, 196, 242, 258, 281, 311, 324 and 376) or taxi.

Keshla Bazaar

You'll find this colourful indoor-outdoor market just next to the new Metkarting Centre in Ganjlik. Vendors sell a good range of fresh produce. Bring your camera during watermelon and pomegranate season for some fantastic shots of car boots turned into grocery stands. 63-69 Aliyar Aliyev St, Narimanov. **Metro** Ganjlik

May 28th Bazaar

Located underground at the 28th of May Metro, you will find a thriving market selling clothes, jewellery, watches, books, swimwear, toys and some homewares. Prices are reasonable. This is a great place to shop during the hot summer months, as it is markedly cooler than any outdoor bazaar. Azadliq & Fizuli Kubinka. **Metro** 28th of May

Nasimi Bazaar

This market has a nice selection of flowers for sale year-round, in addition to a small produce and meat section. You'll also find home items and children's toys. Block 90 Azadliq Ave, Nasimi. **Metro** Ganjlik

Teze Bazaar

This is one of the largest and most popular bazaars in the city, although its central location means that prices are a little higher than elsewhere. It houses a large fresh produce section, butchers and several rows of household goods, tools and electronics. Teze Bazaar is one of the best places to buy fresh lamb (although be sure to check it for freshness, as the meat is not refrigerated) and there are some fantastic dried fruit vendors. Caviar is also available, but prices are high. 73 Samed Vurgun St, Nasimi. **Metro** Nizami or 28th of May

Yashil (Green) Bazaar

Although the Yashil Bazaar carries many of the same products as other city markets, you can usually find them here for a fraction of the price. A kilo of broccoli, for example, will cost a third of the price of other bazaars. You can also find hard-to-come-by produce such as coconut, pineapple and avocado on a regular basis. Khatai Prospect, Nr Neymat Guliyev & Firdovsi Mammadov St, Narimanov. **Metro** 28th of May

Shopping

Shopping Malls & Department Stores

From the latest international fashions to Soviet era wigs, there is much to discover in the malls and department stores of Baku.

If you're a true mall enthusiast, you won't want to miss Park Bulvar (www.parkbulvar.az). It's the newest and most glitzy mall in Baku, located on the prestigious seaside Boulevard and populated with high-end international shops. It also has a great range of high street fashion stores, including the likes of Mango, Coast, Nine West and Benetton, as well as a Debenhams department store. There's also a food court, children's play area, bowling alley and cinema. Although most items here are on the costly side, you'll find slashed prices during sales periods and some good bargains to boot.

Park Bulvar has paved the way for more glamorous shopping malls, and there are several ambitious projects currently underway. The Jale Shopping Centre in downtown Baku, Palmira Shopping Centre and the Railway Retail Centre (near 28th of May Metro) are all currently in various stages of construction. The Flame Towers, three stunning buildings which reach over 30 storeys high, are already changing the Baku skyline. Although the design is inspired by the country's Zoroastrian past, it's also clearly a statement of Azerbaijan's future ambitions. This $350 million project is slated for completion in 2011, and will include a large retail centre. Prior to these new arrivals, the mall culture in Baku was fairly limited, but there are several small centres throughout the city that house mainly local boutiques, as well as a few international brand stores.

Nargiz Plaza (012 496 88 22) and Khagani Centre (012 498 8564) are both located near Fountain Square. Nargiz Plaza has several international brands, including L'Occitane En Provence, Orchestra and Puma. The third floor houses Dalida Café which has a lovely rooftop terrace overlooking Fountain Square. The Khagani Centre has fewer brand stores but you might find some hidden gems. The first floor is a good place to pick up costume jewellery, while there are some nice gift shops on the second floor. Sahil Shopping Center (012 498 0106) is located above the Sahil Metro and houses numerous costume jewellery and dress shops.

There are a couple of big department stores in town. In the new Park Bulvar mall is a Debenhams (www.debenhams.com). Spread across two floors is a great selection of men's, women's and children's clothes in addition to handbags, swimwear, and accessories. Although the sticker prices are marked up from the UK, they are slashed by up to 70% during sales. When it comes to department stores, any serious shopper has to take a trip to MUM, the landmark Soviet-era shop (012 494 4390). Each major city in the Soviet Union had a central department store where a whole range of goods were sold, but capitalism has injected a few more choices at today's MUM. At this behemoth store, you'll find just about everything and anything, including jewellery, watches, electronics, textiles, cosmetics and even wigs. It is located at the corner of Azerbaijan Prospect and Nizami Street, just behind Fountain Square.

Going Out

Dine, Drink, Dance	156
Entertainment	162
Venue Directory	166
Area Directory	170
Restaurants & Cafes	174
Bars & Clubs	192

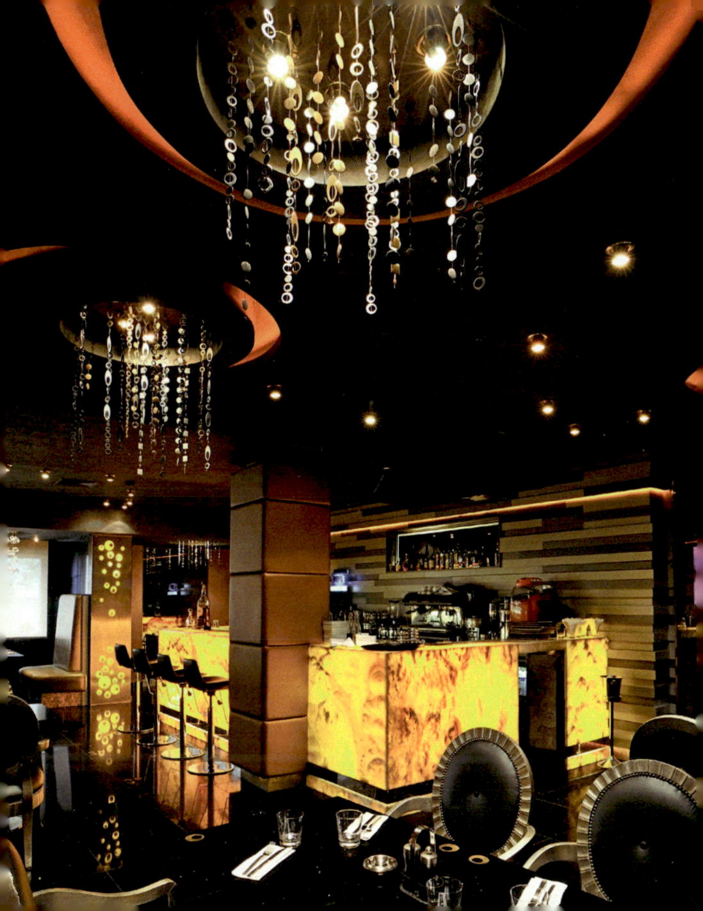

Going Out

Dine, Drink, Dance

With good authentic food, a burgeoning bar scene and plenty of party options, you can have a ball in Baku.

Baku is a very tolerant city, and the going out scene is a lively one. There is no shortage of decent restaurants, serving up a variety of local and international cuisine, and after you've eaten, there is an ever-expanding choice of late-night lounge bars and clubs to explore.

Within the capital a great array of dining options can be found covering everything from European to Middle Eastern and south-east Asian – and of course, the delightfully fresh tasting food of the Caucasus. As is the case with shopping, at the high end, the Baku restaurant scene is all about style (sometimes over content), which

Wines

Azeri wines are improving all the time and, with the lack of stringent import tax meaning they generally cost around half as much as a bottle of average imported plonk, can be extremely appealing. Generally speaking, the reds are better than the whites, with the Ganja and Ismailli regions producing the best grapes. Western palates should probably avoid the sweet and semi-dry options, while the dry bottles are really surprisingly good.

inevitably means that the prices can be on the hefty side in some of the more swanky establishments. But there are some good mid-range options too, as well as some real local gems to be found.

Many bars in the busy downtown area south of Fountain Square also have kitchens attached that offer good, cheap fodder, so this is the area to explore if you are trying to keep costs down. More expensive restaurants, serving excellent food of all cuisine types, are spread across the city, with many clustered around this same downtown area and in the Hyatt district of Nasimi.

Generally speaking, Fridays and Saturdays are the busiest nights and booking at weekends is always advisable, while some of the more costly places tend to be quiet on midweek evenings – meaning you can get a table easily enough, but the atmosphere might not be the liveliest.

Unlike the non-secular Islamic states in the region, alcohol is freely available in Azerbaijan. Baku's development over recent years has seen the bar scene blossom, and upscale bars and booming clubs have sprung up all over town, to complement the more dated selection of down and dirty expat pubs –

> **Opening Hours**
> Most restaurants and bars in Baku are open seven days a week and from 11:00 until well after midnight. Many venues will tell you they close 'at last customer' which really means that they will close on a quiet night, but are happy to stay open if there is trade.

although what these places lack in terms of finesse, they can more than make up for on the bonhomie score.

Cocktail Bars

Most bars and cafes have a cocktail list, but the level of mixology in many is variable. The best places to go for cocktails remain the big hotel bars which often come with a view to match. The best of the best in hotel land are The Sky Bar (p.202) at the Landmark; Azza Bar (012 498 2402) at ISR Plaza's Radisson Blu and Mirvari (012 490 6000) at the Park Inn.

Outside of hotel land, Chinar (p.176) has a wonderful selection of far and away the best and most unusual cocktails in town, while Mesa Lounge (012 598 8866) and Kishmish (012 492 9182) come in a little way behind. There is also building excitement that there will be some impressive new joints in town with the glut of new five-star hotels set to open in the capital soon (see p.58).

Vegetarian Food

Although the concept of vegetarianism is an

Tea Houses

Azerbaijan is a tea-drinking culture, and tea houses, or 'çay evi' are everywhere in Baku and around the country, usually only charging up to 50 qapiks or so a head for a small pot of tea, always served in a glass and with accompanying sweets. The precise line up of sweets varies considerably, of course, and is best experienced at Kishmish (012 492 9182) in the Old City.

alien one to most Azeris, there is a surprising amount of vegetarian-friendly fare available, particularly if you eat dairy and eggs. While the quality of local vegetables is extremely good and the produce very tasty, vegans may get a little weary of endless bunches of raw, undressed herbs and vegetables, although many of the new wave of European-style cafes have very decent salad menus on offer. Azeri, Lebanese, Persian and other Middle Eastern places generally serve excellent vegetarian mezze dishes alongside their meat-heavy mains, and the few good Indian kitchens are used to catering for vegetarians too.

Street Food

The ubiquitous schawarma, or schaorma, is, as throughout the Middle East, the staple street food of Azerbaijan and often ordered by bread-type; for example, a 'lavash' is a kebab wrapped in a soft, pitta-like bread and served with sauce and salad. Shawarma Number 1 (p.188) on Nizami Street is considered by many to be the best place for street food in Baku, the majority of the rest being clustered around 28th of May and Sahil Metros and all are just as insalubrious as they look. A stroll along the Boulevard will reveal another curious Bakuvian street food obsession – candy floss, sold from the numerous concessions along the seafront and enjoyed by promenading locals.

Eat Azeri

Azeri cuisine is excellent, when prepared properly and in a restaurant with enough custom to ensure a wide selection of dishes are available. Some of the best national cuisine is prepared at the Old City Restaurant (012 492 0555), near the south western Old City gate that leads onto the Boulevard.

If you would rather sample Azeri specialities in a more modern surrounding, then head to Zeytun (which means 'olive' in Azeri) on the fourth floor of Park Bulvar (012 493 3587). If ambience is all, however, then the Old City's beautiful, ancient Karavan Saray (p.184), and The Mugham Club (p.186), should be your first ports of call. Here the food is undeniably good but it is the setting that is unforgettable. The authentic Azeri atmosphere at both is truly outstanding and, in the case of the latter, your dinner will be accompanied by a stunning display of traditional music and dance as well. These really are dining experiences not to be missed during your time in Baku.

Karaoke

Karaoke is something of an obsession in Baku and many bars sport a karaoke screen or two or, in certain cases, twelve. Best of the best include the Pride Karaoke Lounge (012 493 5308, 1 Natavan St), where you can perform in front of the whole bar on a stage, under a spotlight, and Studio 2 (012 598 4241, 4 U.Hadjibeyov St), which features sofa-lined booths and private suites, complete with fish tank coffee tables and the longest list of songs, in six languages, anywhere in town.

Going Out

Going Out — Entertainment

Cinemas

Much to the delight of the English-speaking expat population of Baku, the brand new cinema at Park Bulvar shopping mall (012 493 3587) is the first in Azerbaijan to feature a regular programme of English language films. The cinema features six screens, three of which have 3D capabilities; shows times are listed on www.bakucitylife.com.

The grand old Azerbaijan cinema (8 Aziz Aliyev St, www.cinema.az), as well as all the other cinemas, mainly show films in Azeri or Russian. For a novel viewing experience, cruise along to the brand new Royal Cinema drive-in movie screen in the Ramstore carpark on Babak Avenue. You can tune in your radio to pick up the movie's sound and enjoy the film while munching popcorn in the comfort of your own car. Showtimes are listed on the Royal Cinema Facebook page. If you want an even larger than life experience, try the new 12 seat 4D cinema at the National Seaside Park (aka the Boulevard), where you can watch short films enhanced by smell and feel. For an extra dimension, there are even 5D movies being shown here too.

Concerts & Live Music

There are a variety of music concerts staged in Baku throughout the year. Jazz is the most popular genre, and well-known local and international acts come to town to play at the many venues and at the annual jazz festival (see box).To find out more about the country's strong jazz pedigree, a good place to start is the Jazz In Azerbaijan Anthology, a double CD and book set that is available from the main music stores in Baku (see p.142).

Mugham, or mugam, is the classical music of Azerbaijan (added to the UNESCO representative list of intangible cultural heritage of humanity in 2003), and concerts take place at the new International Mugham Centre (012 437 0030, www.mugam.az) on the Boulevard, and at smaller venues such as the Mugham Club (p.186). The European classical music scene is also particularly impressive and seasons of concerts at the Philharmonic Hall (p.94) are hugely popular and advertised on billboards around Baku. Fans of the Russian and Turkish pop and rap music scenes are unlikely to be disappointed, with big names from Moscow and Istanbul playing some of the more prestigious clubs and venues with some regularity.

> ### Baku Jazz
>
> **The annual International Baku Jazz Festival has been staged at various times of the year but in 2010 was in October at the Baku Jazz Center and some of the city's other main entertainment venues.**
>
> **Outside of the festival, the Baku Jazz Center (p.193), located on Rashid Behbudov Street, has a year-round programme of events; see www.jazzcenter.jazz.az for details. Other venues worth checking to see what's on or just heading to for the vibe include the Face Club (p.197), Heydar Aliyev Palace (p.92), Opera Lounge (012 418 0660) and Azza Bar (012 498 2402).**

Some major pop acts have graced Baku with their presence in recent years, with artists of the calibre of Elton John performing at the Tofik Bakhramov Stadium (p.126), while the likes of Kelly Rowland have played Heydar Aliyev Palace. The Open Air or Green Theatre (012 492 49 82, Sonakhanim Velikhanli St) is usually headlined by Turkish acts, while Russian hip-hop and Moscow DJs tend toward the Hezz (012 510 6600) and Face Club (p.197). Chinar (p.176) played host to The Sugababes at its opening. On a smaller scale, many of the expat pubs in the downtown area have a weekly live music night, usually with local rock bands or, in the case of Finnegan's (p.197), a surprisingly good folk rock outfit. Check local listings for events on during your visit. Tickets are usually available from the venue in question or from the booth next to Cafe Mozart on A. Alizadeh Street.

Theatre

The theatre is popular in Baku, with a range of plays and shows being staged year-round at various venues in town. The downside to non-native speakers though is that the performances are almost always in Azeri or Russian, so you will be going for the experience of the lavish productions rather than the prose. The main exceptions to this are of course the operas and ballets, which can be followed (or not) whatever your main language. Main venues include the Opera and Ballet Theatre on Nizami Street (p.147), Philharmonic Hall on Istiglaliyyat Street (p.147), and the Musical Comedy Theatre on Azerbaijan Avenue (p.146).

Going Out

Entertainment

Going Out

Venue Directory

Cafes & Restaurants

American	Sunset Cafe	p.189
Asian	Chinar	p.176
	Shilla	p.188
	Spice Inn	p.188
Azeri	Bah Bah	p.175
	Firuze	p.180
	Karavan Saray	p.184
	Mugham Club	p.186
	Penjere	p.187
Cafe/Coffee Shop	Ali & Nino Cafe	p.174
	Araz Cafe	p.174
	Aroma Cafe	p.175
	Chocolate Café	p.178
	Cottage Cafe	p.178
	Duplex Cafe	p.179
	Gourmet Shop	p.180
	Gubernator Cafe	p.180
	Marco Polo	p.186
	Park Bulvar Food Court	p.187
	Shawarma No 1	p.188
	Traveller's Cafe	p.190
Chinese	Hong Kong	p.182
	Lotus	p.185
European	Cafe City	p.176
	Cafe Mozart	p.176
	Dalida	p.179
	Zeytun	p.190
Far Eastern	Jasmine & Siam	p.183

Georgian	Georgian House	p.180
	Imereti	p.183
	U Dali	p.190
German	Paul's	p.187
Indian	Bombay Palace	p.175
	Maharajah	p.185
International	Hazz Cafe	p.182
	The Grill	p.182
Italian	Cafe Caramel	p.176
	Finestra	p.179
	Il Gusto	p.182
	Il Mosaico	p.183
	La Strada	p.184
	La Taverna	p.184
	Scalini	p.188
	Trattoria La Olivia	p.189
Japanese	Chio Chio San	p.178
	Mado	p.185
	Zakura Bar & Dining	p.190
Lebanese	Beyrut	p.175
Mexican	Mexicana	p.186
Pizzeria	Pizza Inn	p.187
Steakhouse	Churasao Steak House	p.178
Turkish	Anadolu 1	p.174
	Izmir	p.183
	Mangal BBQ	p.185
	Sultan's	p.189

Going Out

Venue Directory

Bars, Pubs & Clubs

Bars

3 Bears	p.192
Avalon	p.192
Bells	p.193
Beluga Bar	p.193
Champion's Sports Bar	p.194
City Lights Bar	p.194
Clansman	p.196
Corner Bar	p.196
Harry's Bar	p.197
Konti Bar	p.198
Living Room	p.198
Madonna	p.198
Marshall's	p.199
Old Forester	p.200
Phoenix Bar	p.200
Refresh Bar	p.200
Room Bar	p.201
Saloon Bar	p.201
Shakespeare's	p.201
Shark Bar	p.201
Sky Bar	p.202
Stranger's	p.202
Sultan Inn	p.202
Tequila Junction	p.203
The Brewery	p.193
The Caledonia	p.194
Top Bar	p.203
Tortuga Pirate Bar	p.203

Clubs	Vertigo Bar	p.203
	Baku Jazz Center	p.193
	Cross Roads	p.196
	Face	p.197
	Infiniti	p.198
	Metkarting	p.199
Pubs	Adam's Sports Bar	p.192
	Corona Pub	p.196
	Finnegan's	p.197
	Red Lion	p.200
	The Britannia	p.194

Going Out

Going Out

Area Directory

Nasimi

Restaurant

Chio Chio San	Dilara Aliyeva St	p.178
Georgian House	4 28 May St	p.180
Gourmet Shop	1 Bakikhanov St	p.180
Il Gusto	7 Gogol St	p.182
Jasmine & Siam	6 Bakikhanov St	p.183
La Strada	206 Dilara Aliyeva St	p.184
Scalini	2 Bakikhanov St	p.188
Shawarma No 1	Nr Nizami & Gogol Sts	p.188
Shilla	51 Khatai Prospect	p.188
The Grill	Hyatt Regency Baku	p.182
U Dali	Mirza Ibrahimov St	p.190

Bars

3 Bears	Rasul Rza St	p.192
Avalon	Gogol St	p.192
Baku Jazz Center	Nr Rashid Behbudov & Dilara Aliyeva St	p.193
Beluga Bar	Hyatt Regency Baku	p.193
City Lights Bar	ISR Plaza Radisson Hotel	p.194
Corner Bar	Nr Rasul Rza St & Tolstoy St	p.196
Corona Pub	195 Bashir Safaroglu St	p.196
Cross Roads	Tolstoy St, Nr Corner Bar	p.196
Infiniti	148 Vidadi St	p.198
Madonna	Rasul Rza St	p.198
Old Forester	Bashir Safaroglu St	p.200
Refresh Bar	Nr Tolstoy & Rasul Rza Sts	p.200
Stranger's	Rasul Rza St	p.202

Baku Mini **Visitors'** Guide

Tequila Junction	73 Nizami St	p.203
The Britannia	Hyatt Regency Baku	p.194
The Caledonia	Nr Nizami St & Rasul Rza St	p.194
Vertigo Bar	Rasul Rza St	p.203

Old City
Restaurant

Gubernator Cafe	Nr Icheri Sheher Metro Station	p.180
Karavan Saray	11 Gulla St	p.184
Mugham Club	9 Haghigat Rzayeva St	p.186

Bars

Sultan Inn	20 Boyuk Gala St	p.202
Top Bar	Meridian Hotel	p.203

Sabayil
Restaurant

Ali & Nino Cafe	Z Taghiyev St	p.174
Araz Cafe	Fountain Square	p.174
Beyrut	Z Taghiyev St	p.175
Cafe Caramel	7 A Alizadeh St	p.176
Cafe City	Fountain Square	p.176
Cafe Mozart	2 A Alizadeh St	p.176
Chinar	1 Shovket Alekperova St	p.176
Chocolate Café	4 Yusif Mammadaliyev St	p.178
Cottage Cafe	35 Gurban Abbasov St	p.178
Duplex Cafe	1 Ibrahimov St	p.179
Firuze	14 T Aliyarbekov St	p.180
Il Mosaico	14 A Alizadeh St	p.183

www.liveworkexplore.com

Maharajah	6 A Alizadeh St	p.185
Mangal BBQ	11 A Alizadeh St	p.185
Mexicana	17 Taghiyev St	p.186
Pizza Inn	Fountain Square	p.187
Sunset Cafe	8 Aziz Aliyev St	p.189
Trattoria La Olivia	14 Z Taghiyev St	p.189
Zakura Bar & Dining	9 A Alizadeh	p.190
Zeytun	Park Bulvar	p.190

Bars

Adam's Sports Bar	6 A Alizadeh St	p.192
Clansman	9 T Aliyarbeyov St	p.196
Finnegan's	8 A Alizadeh St	p.197
Harry's Bar	8 Z Taghiyev St	p.197
Living Room	17 Z Taghiyev St	p.198
Marshall's	Z Taghiyev St	p.199
Phoenix Bar	10 Y Mammadaliyev St	p.200
Red Lion	Z Taghiyev St	p.200
Room Bar	T Aliyarbeyov St	p.201
Saloon Bar	Z Taghiyev St	p.201
Shakespeare's	A Alizadeh St	p.201
Tortuga Pirate Bar	T Aliyarbeyov St	p.203

Sahil
Restaurant

Anadolu 1	5 Pushkin St	p.174
Aroma Cafe	18 U Hajibekov St	p.175
Bombay Palace	25 Bul Bul Prospect	p.175
Churasao Steak House	14 U Hajibekov St	p.178

Hazz Cafe	Landmark Bldg, Nr Khagani & Nizami Sts	p.182
Imereti	13 Khagani St	p.183
Izmir	68 Nizami St	p.183
Marco Polo	17 Khagani St	p.186
Sultan's	10 Khagani St	p.189
Traveller's Cafe	68 Nizami St	p.190

Bars

Bells	Khagani St	p.193
Champion's Sports Bar	Alley, Nr Nizami & Khagani Sts	p.194
Konti Bar	17 Nizami St	p.198
Shark Bar	Khagani St, Nr Sultan's	p.201
Sky Bar	The Landmark Hotel Baku	p.202

Yasamal

Restaurant

Finestra	14 Nakhchivani St	p.179
Hong Kong	38 Inshaatchilar Prospect	p.182
Lotus	2 B Baghirova St	p.185
Mado	33 Inshaatchilar Prospect	p.185
Paul's	Zargarpalan St	p.187
Penjere	245 Abdullah Shaig St	p.187
Spice Inn	31 Inshaatchilar Ave	p.188

Bars

| Face | 10 Nizami St | p.197 |
| The Brewery | 27 Istiglaliyyat St | p.193 |

Restaurants & Cafes

Going Out

From high-end modern restaurants to atmospheric local eateries and a cafe culture that keeps buzzing day and night, Baku is busy with choice.

Ali & Nino Cafe — Cafe/Coffee Shop
Taghiyev St, Sabayil — 012 493 1530

Across from the bookshop bearing the same name, this cafe boasts a wide range of rich desserts, fancy cocktails, smoothies and teas. The walls are decorated with interesting paintings and photographs depicting characters from the famous Ali and Nino book and images of the Tsarist era. Wi-Fi is available. **Metro** Sahil

Anadolu 1 — Turkish
5 Pushkin St, Sahil — 012 498 8758

This cheap, cheerful diner is great for a quick lunch or casual dinner, serving tasty fare at reasonable prices. The pre-made options are the best value, though a la carte is also available. Anadolu 2 can be found at 5 Rasul Rza St (012 498 6804). **Metro** 28th of May

Araz Cafe — Cafe/Coffee Shop
Fountain Square Sabayil

More of a beer-tent teashop than a cafe, there is some great outdoor seating and it's conveniently located for people watching. This place is also open late, making it perfect for an after-dinner beer as you watch the world go by.

Aroma Cafe
Cafe/Coffee Shop
18 U Hajibekov St, Sahil 012 598 0707
With couch seating upstairs and dining downstairs, this Wi-Fi hotspot is always busy and has a wide range of teas, sweets, cocktails and food. It's a great place for coffee in winter and is conveniently located just down the street from the Sahil Metro station. **Metro** Sahil

Bah Bah
Azeri
Aliyarbekov St, Sabayil 012 498 8734
Just off Fountain Square, this chic yet homely place is a great place to go for Russian and Azeri cuisine. The earthenware dishes are filled to overflowing, and you'll be entertained by the belly dancers and Azeri music as you eat. **Metro** Sahil

Beyrut
Lebanese
Z Taghiyev St, Sabayil 012 598 0665
This reputable Lebanese restaurant serves great food, is a popular lunch spot, and is a good choice for a mid-range evening out. Mezze dishes are great for sharing, and you can really get the Beirut buzz by indulging in a sheesha (hookah) pipe after your meal. **Metro** Sahil

Bombay Palace
Indian
25 Bul Bul Prospect, Sahil 012 493 2446
Located close to the Jazz Center, the Heydar Aliyev Concert Hall and Opera & Ballet Theatre, this Indian eatery is a good option before catching a show. It may be tucked away on a back street, but it's well known and reputable. **Metro** Sahil

www.liveworkexplore.com

Restaurants & Cafes

Cafe Caramel
Italian
7 A Alizadeh St, Sabayil 012 498 9353
This cafe has a great weekend brunch menu and a good range of lunch options. The coffee is good, and the fresh desserts and ice creams are also popular. It's open until late, the prices are fair, and the service is excellent.

Cafe City
European
Fountain Square, Sabayil 012 598 8686
This fashionable eatery has indoor and outdoor seating in a chic new location at Fountain Square, as well as a convenient lunchtime spot on Rashid Behbudov Street (012 598 8833), across from Sahil Baghi Park. The staff are attentive and the meals are tasty and reasonably-priced. **Metro** Icheri Sheher

Cafe Mozart
European
2 A Alizadeh St, Sabayil 012 498 1925
One of the older restaurants in Baku, it's also one of the prime spots for alfresco people-watching. Its Sunday brunch buffet is famous, but it's open for a coffee or a drink all week. The menu is good but service can be below par. **Metro** Sahil

Chinar
Asian
1 Shovket Alekperova St, Sabayil 012 492 0888
Serving good quality Asian fusion fare, the popular Chinar offers small taster menu dishes or platefuls big enough to satisfy the truly hungry. There's a late bar and lounge where you can also order dim sum and sushi – but drinks service can be slow. Bookings advisable. **Metro** Icheri Sheher

Going Out

Restaurants & Cafes

Chio Chio San
Japanese
Dilara Aliyeva St, Nasimi   012 498 0272
Reputed to offer the best sushi in Baku, this elegant mid-priced restaurant, behind the Jazz Club, is a great option for pre-theatre dinners. The interior is a modern variation on traditional Japanese style, with paper screen style walls, black tables, hanging lamps, and an outdoor terrace. **Metro** 28th of May

Chocolate Café
Cafe/Coffee Shop
4 Yusif Mammadaliyev St, Sabayil   012 418 1127
The various branches of this cosy coffee shop chain offer free Wi-Fi, decent coffee and a tasty food menu, including pasta dishes, sandwiches, salads, soups and desserts. Shisha, spirits and wine make it a good spot for an evening drink as well. There's another branch in the Old City at 21 Boyuk Gala Street.
Metro Sahil

Churasao Steak House
Steakhouse
14 U Hajibekov St, Sahil   012 598 5409
This hole-in-the-wall steakhouse is one of Baku's best-kept secrets. Those in the know argue that it serves some of the best steak in town – and when there's live music to go with it, there's many a happy customer. It's just off Molokan Gardens.
Metro Sahil

Cottage Cafe
Cafe/Coffee Shop
35 Gurban Abbasov St, Sabayil   012 497 4830
Located opposite Villa Petrolea, this cafe offers a range of hearty lunches, making it a good alternative to the standard

staff canteen. It's a great spot for a working lunch, or for a casual bite to eat with friends and family.
Metro Sahil

Dalida — European
Nargiz Mall, 3rd Floor Sabayil — 012 496 8804
This chic rooftop restaurant has an enormous terrace overlooking Fountain Square, with comfy couches and cafe-style dining. There's a variety of cocktails and desserts, and the food is pretty good too. The ambience is casual at lunch and slightly dressier in the evening. Open till 01:00.
Metro Icheri Sheher

Duplex Cafe — Cafe/Coffee Shop
1 Ibrahimov St, Sabayil — 012 494 9990
Spread over two floors and located just off Fountain Square, across from the Armenian church, this is a popular spot for lunch or coffee. While the drinks are a little overpriced, the variety of beverages is excellent, and the cafe's small delicatessen does a roaring trade. **Metro** Icheri Sheher

Finestra — Italian
14 Nakhchivani St, Yasamal — 012 436 7854
A tried and tested option, this large, mid-priced restaurant is ideal for big groups. The standard Italian options are all here, including a decent pizza selection, and it's open for both lunch and dinner. There is also regular live entertainment, but be warned that it tends to be a little on the tacky side.
Metro Elmlar Akademiyasi

www.liveworkexplore.com

Firuze
Azeri
14 T Aliyarbekov St, Sabayil 012 493 9634

To find Firuze, walk under the green plastic rain cover, down the steps and into this Azeri cave. It offers great local cuisine, with a wide range of Turkish kebabs and meats, plus a handful of Russian dishes. **Metro** Sahil

Georgian House
Georgian
4 28 May St, Nasimi 012 493 7003

This is probably the best of the Georgian options in Baku. The khachapuri (cheese in pastry with various toppings) is amazing and the range of meat-free dishes makes it a good choice for vegetarians too. The restaurant is on the small side, so be sure to make a reservation. **Metro** Sahil

Gourmet Shop
Cafe/Coffee Shop
1 Bakikhanov St, Nasimi 012 496 1234

This deli counter has lots of imported treats to tickle your taste buds, with everything from goat's cheese to smoked salmon. You can build your own sandwich, which is served with salad for AZN10. There's also creamy chocolaty indulgence to be had at the patisserie counter.

Gubernator Cafe
Cafe/Coffee Shop
Nr Icheri Sheher Metro Station, Old City

This gazebo-like tea shop in the renovated Old City wall park (Gubernator's Park) has an excellent selection of ice cream – just the thing to perk you up and cool you down after a hot day of walking around the Old City. **Metro** Icheri Sheher

Going Out

Restaurants & Cafes

www.liveworkexplore.com

The Grill
International
Hyatt Regency Baku, Nasimi 012 496 1234

The wine list is a bit pricey and the restaurant lacks atmosphere when it's quiet, but there's an excellent range of fish and meat dishes here, and usually a good veggie option too. The kitchen staff will try to whisk up what you're craving if it's not on the menu. **Metro** Nizami

Hazz Cafe
International
Landmark Bldg, Nr Khagani & Nizami Sts, Sahil 012 598 5978

In the lobby of the Landmark complex, this top-end jazz club-cum-cafe is a mellow place for a pot of tea or a decent glass of wine. You'll often catch live music after 20:00, while during the day it caters to both office workers and casual diners. **Metro** 28th of May

Hong Kong
Chinese
38 Inshaatchilar Prospect, Yasamal 012 436 9001

Hong Kong is one of the most popular Chinese restaurants in town, with friendly, English-speaking staff and a wide-ranging menu. The lunch menu starts from AZN12. Beware, the portions are enormous. **Metro** Sahil

Il Gusto
Italian
7 Gogol St, Nasimi 012 494 8318

With a prime downtown location, this long-established Baku eatery is a great option for both lunch and dinner. It has good pizza, the ambiance is warm, and it's good value for money. **Metro** Sahil

Il Mosaico — Italian
14 A Alizadeh St, Sabayil — 012 493 6193

This lovely-looking restaurant is fabulously decorated. There's a nice selection of southern European wines, and its Italian management team means you can expect some authenticity, as well as decent service and food – which includes all the Italian classics.

Imereti — Georgian
13 Khagani St, Sahil — 012 493 4181

Although nothing special from the outside, this place is regarded by many as the best place in Baku for Georgian food. The staff are eccentric but attentive, and there's a great atmosphere. The khingali (Georgian dumplings) are seriously highly recommended. You'll be amazed at the value, and the friendly welcome, but just beware of the potent cha cha (Georgian vodka). **Metro** Sahil

Izmir — Turkish
68 Nizami St, Sahil — 012 493 0273

This cheap and cheerful eatery is a great spot to pick up take-out lunches and other goodies. It's very popular with locals and has quality food for a very reasonable price. Buffet and a la carte menu are both available. **Metro** Sahil

Jasmine & Siam — Far Eastern
6 Bakikhanov St, Nr Hyatt Bridge Plaza, Nasimi — 012 404 5404

Even though this Asian fusion restaurant is out of the way, the ambiance makes it worth the journey. A great view over the surrounding area and attentive service, combined with the generous portions of Thai and Chinese specialities, make this a great top-end choice. **Metro** Nizami

Karavan Saray — Azeri
11 Gulla St, Old City — 012 492 6668

A visit to this traditional Azeri caravanserai, housed in a beautiful old building, is a must. Tables in alcove rooms off a central courtyard are decorated with carpets and crafts. The qutab (flatbread filled with spinach and herbs, lamb or squash), saj (grilled meat with roast vegetables and potatoes), and lula kebabs are all recommended. Live mugham music is usually played. Great value too. **Metro** Icheri Sheher

La Strada — Italian
206 Dilara Aliyeva St, Nasimi — 012 498 2212

There's lots of attention to detail in the decor at this authentic bistro, and the bright, open, airy space makes for a pleasant dining experience. The mushroom risotto is very good, soups are inventively served in bowls made out of bread and the pizzas are both delicious and enormous. **Metro** 28th of May

La Taverna — Italian
Najafbey Vazirov St, Kubinka — 012 440 8698

This little-known gem is probably the best Italian restaurant in Baku. The owner, Sergio, welcomes you warmly, and although the restaurant decor is nothing special, the food is authentic and very good value. The wine list is well-priced, and vegetarians are well catered for.

Lotus Chinese
2 B Baghirova St, Yasamal 012 436 9750

Chinese restaurants in Baku tend to offer some of the most formal dining experiences, with tuxedoed waiters and five-star restaurant prices. Lotus is no exception, the food is simple Chinese fare, with dishes like fried rice and egg rolls – but be prepared to pay for it.

Mado Japanese
33 Inshaatchilar Prospect, Yasamal 012 497 5544

This place serves excellent value lunches and has a good reputation for sushi. Sukiyaki and teppanyaki are both available, and it also serves a selection of Korean dishes. The Sushi Boat is a great choice for large parties, if a little expensive. **Metro** Elmlar Akademiyasi

Maharajah Indian
6 A Alizadeh St, Sabayil 012 492 4334

Located above Shakespeare's Bar, this well-established Baku restaurant is a popular choice at weekends – although the music from below can be a bit distracting. Catering to groups of various sizes, this is a casual place, with great value food, and it has to be a good sign that it is so popular with the local Indian population. **Metro** Sahil

Mangal BBQ Turkish
11 Alizadeh St, Sabayil 012 498 8260

This compact, eclectic place has a huge indoor barbecue and a wide range of interesting dishes. It's a great place for high quality food at low prices. Tuck yourself in at one of its minute tables and order from the tapas-style starters, or go for something more substantial.

Marco Polo
Cafe/Coffee Shop
17 Khagani St, Sahil   012 493 3132

With Italian coffee and a variety of lunch fare, this is a good spot for a quick pit stop. The outdoor seating on the summer terrace looks appealing, but its location close to the noisy traffic of Samed Vurgun Street can sometimes make it a fume-filled experience. **Metro** Sahil

Mexicana
Mexican
17 Taghiyev St, Sabayil   012 498 9096

It's not just the only Mexican in town – this is also the place to go for margaritas. The decor is Latin American, and it has a clean, non-smoky bar with the option of live sports matches. Its booths can seat both couples and groups.
Metro Sahil

Mugham Club
Azeri
9 Haghigat Rzayeva St, Old City   012 492 4085/492 3176

Comparable to Karavan Saray, though much more expensive, this lovely courtyard restaurant is open to the elements in summer, but covered in the chillier months. There's a range of traditional and regional food to try. Sample some fresh pomegranate juice to accompany your bottle of vodka. Live Mugham music and belly dancing complete the experience.
Metro Icheri Sheher

Park Bulvar Food Court Cafe/Coffee Shop
Park Bulvar, Sabayil   012 493 3587
This place isn't a cafe as such, but with a selection of traditional Azeri kebabs, sushi, and Russian and Turkish cuisine, the third floor of the newly opened Park Bulvar mall makes a great oasis from the summer heat.
Metro Sahil

Paul's German
Zargarpalan St, Yasamal   050 502 5507
With lovely outdoor tables for the summer and an inviting interior decked out like a Swiss chalet for winter, this is a popular place year round. Lovely tender fillet steaks come fresh from the barbecue, while the simple menu also includes bratwursts and kebabs. There's a good range of imported German beers too.

Penjere Azeri
245 Abdullah Shaig St, Yasamal   012 510 3700
This is a great little place to experience authentic Azeri food. Staff are friendly and can help decipher the menu. Book a table in the upstairs function room to enjoy your fill of live music and belly dancing while you eat. Close to the Hyatt.

Pizza Inn Pizzeria
Fountain Square, Sabayil   012 493 8216
Right on the edge of Fountain Square, and featuring comfortable outdoor tables, this is a great choice for a coffee, evening drink or a spot of people-watching. The pizza is the

best thing on the menu, but there are a variety of cocktails and Turkish and European snacks as well. **Metro** Sahil

Scalini
Italian
2 Bakikhanov St, Nasimi   012 598 2850

Scalini is something of an expat institution. The service is good and the food reliable but it's a bit on the expensive side these days, especially if you go for dinner instead of lunch. The special Pizza Sundays deal is a better option. **Metro** Nizami

Shawarma No 1
Cafe/Coffee Shop
Nr Nizami Street & Gogol, Nasimi

With its bright red tents and outdoor tables, this is a landmark on Nizami Street. Recently refurbished with comfortable seats, it's a great spot for a drink and a good kebab on a sunny afternoon. There's also a nice ice cream shop in the underground area next door. **Metro** Sahil

Shilla
Asian
51 Khatai Prospect, Nasimi   012 417 0102

This place boasts good quality sushi, authentic Korean food and tabletop barbecues. Lovers of Thai food will be pleased to hear that Shilla's popular old Thai menu looks set to be reinstated in the future. **Metro** Khatai

Spice Inn
Asian
31 Inshaatchilar Ave, Yasamal   012 537 0632

This is one of the few places in town still serving reasonably priced Thai and Indian cuisine. It's a versatile choice for entertaining large groups, and it offers a variety of choices from the extensive menu. Of all the menu options, the curry dishes and breads are particularly good. Reservations are rarely needed.

Sultan's
Turkish
10 Khagani St, Sahil   012 598 0555

Not to be confused with the Sultan Inn in the Old City, this place serves cheap and cheerful light lunches, and there's a mid-range menu in the evening. The food is simple, fresh and delicious, and shisha (hookah) pipes often make an after-dinner appearance. There's an open-air restaurant in summer, and a children's play area. **Metro** Sahil

Sunset Cafe
American
8 Aziz Aliyev St, Nr M Rasul-Zadeh St, Sabayil   012 492 2292

Located underneath the Azerbaijan Cinema, this classy yet unpretentious diner is named after the famous Hollywood strip – and is fittingly decorated with an assortment of music and movie star posters. It's popular for coffee and brunch, and a great choice for burgers and desserts. **Metro** Sahil

Trattoria La Olivia
Italian
14 Z Taghiyev St, Sabayil   012 493 0954

This place has a large menu featuring some good classic options, including delicious homemade ravioli. The service from friendly staff is reliable and attentive. The decor is faux-rustic and there's also a sushi bar downstairs which is open till late. **Metro** Sahil

Going Out

Restaurants & Cafes

Traveller's Cafe
Cafe/Coffee Shop
68 Nizami St, Sahil   012 493 2024
Opening at 08:00, this is your best bet for an early weekend coffee. There's a huge list of teas, coffees and hot chocolates and a good selection of food for brunches, as well as desserts.
Metro Sahil

U Dali
Georgian
Mirza Ibrahimov St, Nasimi
Tucked away in a basement on a small backstreet, this is an alternative Georgian restaurant to Imereti. Although the decor is very simple, there are cosy wooden-benched booths behind (optional) curtains, and a delicious traditional khachapuri (cheese pie) features among the assorted Georgian foods.

Zakura Bar & Dining
Japanese
9 Alizade, Sabayil   012 498 1818
The concept at this Japanese joint is izakaya. The decor is stylish, featuring two sleek, modern levels and atmospheric lantern lighting, but the service can be a bit hit and miss. Alcohol is pricey. **Metro** Sahil

Zeytun
European
Park Bulvar, Sabayil   012 598 7420
This chic new restaurant is on the third floor of Park Bulvar and offers fine dining inside or a balcony hookah lounge. It may be located in a shopping mall, but it calls for pretty smart attire and is well worth dressing up for. **Metro** Sahil

Going Out

Restaurants & Cafes

Going Out

Bars & Clubs

From rough and ready expat pubs to high-rise, high-class cocktail bars, Baku's nightlife is calling.

3 Bears — Bar
Rasul Rza St, Nasimi   012 598 0182
Right on the corner of Nizami Street and Rasul Rza, the location of this bar can't be beaten. It's also a nice quiet place for a drink as it rarely gets busy, catering instead to a smattering of Baku regulars. **Metro** Sahil

Adam's Sports Bar — Pub
6 A Alizadeh St, Sabayil   012 498 1289
You'll have no trouble finding someone at this expat haunt to challenge to a game of pool or to have a pint with at the bar while you're in town. There's a superb Indian menu – try the thali (veggie or meat) for a little taste of everything. Wednesday night is buffet night. Open late every day.

Avalon — Bar
Nr Shawarma No 1, Gogol St, Nasimi   055 640 7733
For pool and beer with occasional live music, this is a cosy spot for a drink and a great choice for a meal too. The interior is kitted out in friendly pub decor, and it's recently been redecorated, making it a pleasant place to while away a few hours. **Metro** Sahil

Baku Jazz Center
Nightclub
Nr Rashid Behbudov & Dilara Aliyeva St, Nasimi   012 493 9941
Featuring daily concerts from 21:00, this place has the appropriately dark and smoky ambiance of a jazz club. Food and drinks are nothing to get excited about as the music's the real draw. Shows finish by about 23:00. **Metro** 28th of May

Bells
Bar
Khagani St, Sahil   012 498 5700
This place is popular with locals and has karaoke, shisha, chic decor and occasional live music among its list of attractions. It's the ideal place if you're looking for somewhere to settle back in a booth with friends and enjoy the vibe.
Metro Sahil

Beluga Bar
Bar
Hyatt Regency Baku, Nasimi   012 496 1234
With its location on the pool terrace of the Hyatt, this cocktail bar has a mix of Hyatt gym members, hotel guests and post-work drinkers. While it's not a late-night venue, it can be a great place to stop for a poolside vodka.   **Metro** Nizami

The Brewery
Bar
27 Istiglaliyyat St, Yasamal   012 437 2868
The light, medium and dark beer served at this place is brewed on the premises, and is some of the best ale around. There's a bar menu, a German-themed restaurant, occasional live music, and Oktoberfest celebrations each year.

Bars & Clubs

The Britannia
Pub
Hyatt Regency Baku, Nasimi   012 496 1234
A British themed pub in the Hyatt Regency hotel, The Britannia was one of the first venues in Baku to be popular with expats and it remains a firm favourite with local office workers for an after-work drink. **Metro** Nizami

The Caledonia
Bar
Nr Nizami St & Rasul Rza St, Nasimi
This cosy expat haunt is brimming with Scottish memorabilia. There's also a pool table, good camaraderie and you're sure to find some new mates to watch a sports game with. It's very centrally located and easy to find. **Metro** Sahil

Champion's Sports Bar
Bar
Alley, Nr Nizami St & Khagani St, Sahil   012 562 7526
Tucked away from the main drag, this place is well lit with a large dance floor and a regular live band at weekends. There's a large screen TV in each booth to keep sports junkies happy, and a decent menu for a post-match feed. Sunday night is Latino night. **Metro** Sahil

City Lights Bar
Bar
ISR Plaza Radisson Hotel, Nasimi   012 598 1133
This is a great place to go for drinks, especially on a warm summer evening, thanks to its spectacular panoramic view over Baku. The bar sometimes has a singer, accompanied by live piano and violin, and when you've had your fill of cocktails, the restaurant is right next door. **Metro** Sahil

Going Out

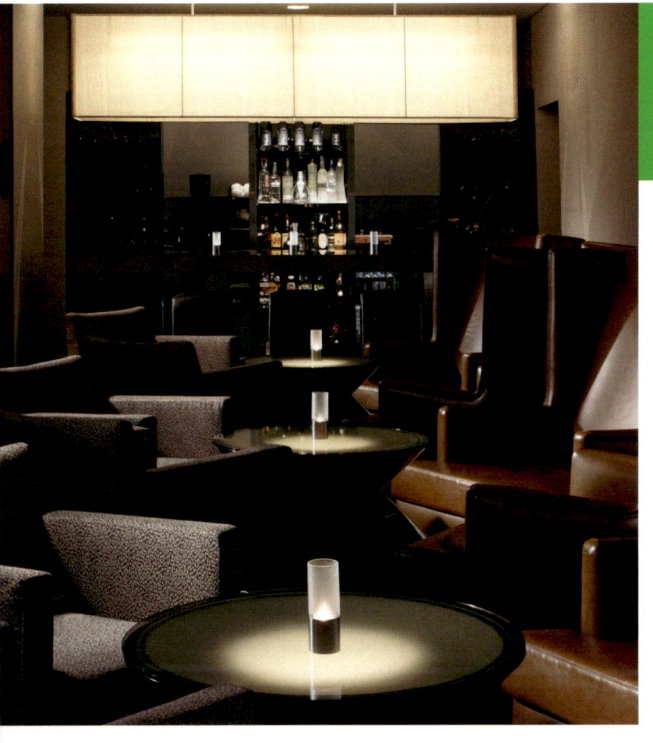

Bars & Clubs

Bars & Clubs

Clansman
Bar
9 T Aliyarbeyov St, Sabayil 012 598 4621
Hidden behind white windows, this brightly lit Scottish centre, in the Fountain Square area, has a friendly crowd of regulars. The bar is spacious and a good place for a pint and a chat. A note to all Glaswegians – on match day, this is firmly a Rangers establishment. **Metro** Sahil

Corner Bar
Bar
Nr Rasul Rza St & Tolstoy St, Nasimi 012 494 8955
This compact joint has regular live music and is a popular after-dinner drinking spot. It might not be the most salubrious of bars, but with European wines and everyone's favourite Irish stout on tap, there's enough to keep most people happy. **Metro** Sahil

Corona Pub
Pub
195 Bashir Safaroglu St, Nasimi 012 494 4301
Whether it's a game of pool or a mellow pint you're after, this backstreet spot is a great place to head if you're looking for a late drink – and rather conveniently, it's usually open till the last person leaves.

Cross Roads
Nightclub
Tolstoy St, Nr Corner Bar, Nasimi
This is THE place to head if you're out very late in Baku, with possibly the best European-style clubbing experience in the city. It's sweaty, crowded and sometimes a little sleazy, but

it plays the latest house and pop music for a die-hard crowd of locals and expats who like to party hard. Open until 05:00. **Metro** Sahil

Face   Nightclub
10 Nizami St, Yasamal   012 497 4471
This recently opened venue has become the haunt of the rich and feckless youth of Baku – though you'll also find a fair few wealthy businessmen and top brass officials, as well as some expats. The drinks are extraordinarily expensive and entry costs upwards of AZN40. The music is a cross between Euro-house and Turkish/Azeri pop, with occasional 90s house and classic rave thrown in to mix things up a bit.

Finnegan's   Pub
8 Alizadeh St, Sabayil   012 498 6564
This traditional Irish pub is one of the earliest opening nightspots in Baku. It's a popular expat joint, with a tempting menu and excellent weekend brunches. The atmosphere is particularly good on Wednesday and Saturday nights when live bands play. Happy Hour is from 19:00-20:00. **Metro** Sahil

Harry's Bar   Bar
8 Z Taghiyev St, Sabayil   050 374 0223
This underground bar, in the Fountain Square area, has a popular pool table where you'll always find a keen opponent. The couches at the other end have enough space for small groups. Can get quite smoky. **Metro** Sahil

Bars & Clubs

Infiniti
Nightclub
148 Vidadi St & Mardanov Brothers Crossroad, Nasimi
012 596 3229

This nightclub has a notorious reputation for attracting 'ladies of the night' and their customers. The good music makes it a fun place for a dance if you're in a large group, but smaller parties might be put off by unwanted attention.

Konti Bar
Bar
17 Nizami St, Sahil
012 498 9191

The Konti Bar has self-service beer taps at the table. Each tap has a counter displaying how much your party has consumed. Most people who have visited have wild stories of nights here involving the consumption of inconceivable volumes of beer.
Metro 28th of May

Living Room
Bar
17 Z Taghiyev St, Sabayil
012 493 8725

Just north of Fountain Square, this place is popular with a young crowd of expats and locals. As well as the standard music there's also karaoke for when the Dutch courage takes hold, as well as a VIP room if you're a bit special. **Metro** Sahil

Madonna
Bar
Rasul Rza St, Nasimi

Madonna is one of the many small bars just north of the crossroads on Rasul Rza. This place is popular late at night and is open from 19:00 until 04:00. There's a pool table, but the bar can get rather smoky in winter. **Metro** Sahil

Marshall's — Bar
Z Taghiyev St, Sabayil — 012 493 7849

This bar has a good Indian menu (though it offers other cuisine too), a large dance floor, and live music on Friday nights. There's a spacious interior, complete with pool table, bar and spaces for both eating and dancing. **Metro** Sahil

Metkarting — Nightclub
1993 A Aliyev St, Ganjlik — 012 564 3322

Not your average disco, Metkarting's outdoor and indoor dancefloors are surrounded by a go-kart track, billiard tables, a swimming pool and lounge beds. You might encounter go-go dancers, a foam party, or DJs spinning Russian, French, and Turkish tunes. Reserve a VIP table near the dance floor, smoke a shisha and dance until dawn. **Metro** Ganjlik

Going Out — Bars & Clubs

Going Out — **Bars & Clubs**

Old Forester
Bar
Bashir Safaroglu St, Nr Citimart, Nasimi 012 598 1932
This clean, up-market place caters for both Azeri families and expat happy-hour groups. With live music and cosy pub decor in a spacious venue, it offers a non-smoky, clean-cut alternative place for a civilised drink. **Metro** 28th of May

Phoenix Bar
Bar
10 Y Mammadaliyev St, Sabayil 070 333 3031
This friendly bar in the Fountain Square area is often the spot for expat gatherings and pub quizzes. It has a pool table, sports coverage, good cocktails and regular live bands, although the neighbours periodically complain about the noise. **Metro** Sahil

Red Lion
Pub
Z Taghiyev St, Sabayil 012 598 3358
This British themed L-shaped bar has a band area at one end and a pool table at the other. It feels a little like you're drinking in a tunnel, but it has a lively scene and shows major sporting events. **Metro** Sahil

Refresh Bar
Bar
Nr Tolstoy & Rasul Rza Sts, Nasimi
This tiny bar underneath Cross Roads nightclub on Tolstoy Street gets busy late at night. It's particularly popular with expats, and has been known to have the bartenders dancing on the bar. **Metro** Sahil

Room Bar — Bar
T Aliyarbeyov St, Sabayil — 050 322 1133

Opposite the Tortuga bar and The Clansman, this petite Turkish bar has a band playing every night. It can get quite smoky late at night and at weekends, but it's quiet before 21:00 and during the week. The place is small, with an intimate feel.

Saloon Bar — Bar
Z Taghiyev St, Sabayil

This cheap and cheerful bar in the Fountain Square area is a great place for a game of pool. It's probably the only underground bar in Baku with an automatic sliding glass door – something to remember when leaving at the end of the night! **Metro** Sahil

Shakespeare's — Bar
A Alizadeh St, Sabayil — 012 498 9121

Another well-frequented expat haunt, but with the drawback that it's very brightly lit, which, if you're there in the early hours, kills the atmosphere somewhat. It shows a range of sports on big screens and has regular live music. Maharajah (p.185), upstairs, serves good Indian food. **Metro** Sahil

Shark Bar — Bar
Khagani St, Nr Sultan's, Sahil — 012 493 9669

Although it's changed location a few times, the underground Shark Bar is an established Baku favourite with cheerful happy hours, a pool table and mirrored walls. Its latest incarnation is just next door to the newly opened Molakan Gardens and Sultan's Restaurant. **Metro** Sahil

Sky Bar Bar
The Landmark Hotel Baku, Sahil 012 465 2000
With floor to ceiling windows and a spectacular view of Baku bay, this 19th storey bar is a showstopper. It features comfy couches, live piano music, 'English Teatime' and a 'Chocoholic Buffet' in the afternoons, and a wide range of coffee, cocktails and tea. There's also a sushi bar on the 21st floor, and Asian restaurant Shin-Shin on the 20th floor.
Metro 28th of May

Stranger's Bar
Rasul Rza St, Nasimi 050 541 0626
With its wood-panelled interior, this cosy place is great for a weekend brunch, a game of darts or pool, or a nightcap. A private entrance prevents curious passers-by from peering in, giving the place an exclusive feel. **Metro** Sahil

Sultan Inn Bar
20 Boyuk Gala St, Old City 012 437 2305
The rooftop bar at this small hotel has amazing views over the Old City, Maiden's Tower and Baku Bay. With great cocktails and a AZN12 business lunch deal, this is an affordable option on a weekday – but prices are higher away from the lunch deal and evening and weekend visits warrant a special occasion. The menu has a French feel. **Metro** Icheri Sheher

Tequila Junction
Bar

73 Nizami St, Nasimi 012 498 4332

This compact little bar is pretty cramped, but it's popular with expats from North America. There's a pool table and a bar bites menu, and there are also a handful of chairs outside on the pavement, which provide a decent spot to watch the world go by from.

Top Bar
Bar

Meridian Hotel, 39 A Zeynalli St, Old City 012 498 1289

The bar adjoining the City View Restaurant at the Meridian Hotel is a good option for a quick drink and has great views over the Old City. Downstairs in the hotel, is a cool, quirky, cave-like bar, which is rarely crowded and features a pool table. **Metro** Icheri Sheher

Tortuga Pirate Bar
Bar

T Aliyarbeyov St, Sabayil 050 405 0778

This brightly lit, cheerful place has interesting, if bizarre, pirate-themed decor. There's a restaurant towards the back, and spacious table, bar and couch seating around a pool table.

Vertigo Bar
Bar

Rasul Rza St, Nasimi 012 596 2512

This small bar has a pool table and is often open to the street, offering a slightly less smoke-filled environment. Frequented by a mix of locals and expats, it's a nice place for a drink, though you'll have to look elsewhere for food. **Metro** Sahil

www.liveworkexplore.com

Index

#
3 Bears Bar	192
8 Kilometre Bazaar	149

A
Absheron	21,105
Absheron Gallery	84
Active Baku	114
Activities	114, 122
Adam's Sports Bar	192
AF Hotel Aqua Park	64
Airlines	32
Airport	30
Airport Transfer	33
Alcohol	157
Ali & Nino Cafe	174
Ali Shamshir's Gallery	84
Aliyev Family	10
Ambassador Hotel	58
Amburan Beach Club	122
Anadolu 1	174
Annual Events	50
Aqua Park	118
Araz Cafe	174
Architecture	28, 76
Areas To Shop	130
Aroma Cafe	175
Around The City	82
Art	136
Art Galleries	66, 84
Art Gallery Vitru	85
Ateshgah	6, 21
ATMs	45
Attractions	66
Austin Hotel	60
Avalon	192
Azcot	60
Azerbaijan	4, 16, 29
Azerbaijan Airlines	30
Azerbaijan Prospect	146
Azerbaijan State Philharmonia	94
Azerbaijan State Puppet Theatre	92
Azeri Cuisine	12, 159
Azeri Opera	93

B
Bah Bah	175
Baku	18
Baku Entertainment Center	119
Baku Hotels	58
Baku Jazz Center	193
Baku Jazz Festival	163
Baku Olympic Stadium	128
Baku's Origins	8
Baku-Tbilisi-Ceyhan Pipeline	10
Balaban	142
Bargaining	134
Bars	154
Battles	8
Bazaars	148
Beach Hotels	64
Beaches	66, 100
Bells	193
Beluga Bar	193
Best Of Baku	28
Beyrut	175
BMI	30
Bombay Palace	175
Botanical Gardens	82, 96
Bottega Veneta	140
Boulvard, The	27, 72, 146
Boutique Palace	60
Bowling	124
Boyuk Gala 19 Art Gallery	136
Brewery, The	193
Britannia, The	194
Brothers' Carpet	138

Index

Bus	52
Buying In Baku	130
Bvlgari	140

C

Cafe Caramel	176
Cafe City	176
Cafe Mozart	176
Cafes	154, 174
Caledonia, The	194
Car Rental	57
Caravanserai	23, 24
Carpet	24, 137
Carpet Museum	24, 28, 88
Caspian Sea	19
Caspian Waterfront	72
Caucasus	4, 5
Centre For Contemporary Art	85
Champion's Sports Bar	194
Chinar	176
Chio Chio San	178
Chocolate Café	178
Christian Dior	132
Christianity	6
Churasao Steak House	178
Cinemas	162
City Lights Bar	194
Clansman	196
Climate	38
Club Oasis	119
Club Olympus	120
Clubs	154
Cocktail Bars	158
Concerts	162
Corner Bar	196
Corniche	72
Corona Pub	196
Cottage Cafe	178
Crescent Beach Hotel & Leisure Resort	64
Crime	38
Cross Roads	196
Culture	6, 10
Customs	33

D

Dalida	179
Dargah Carpet Center	138
Debenhams	152
Department Stores	153
Disabilities	45
Dos & Don'ts	36
Downtown	80
Drugs	39
Duplex Cafe	179
Duty Free	34

E

Early Azerbaijan	6
Economy	16
Electricity	40
Emergency	39
Entertainment	92, 154
Eurovision Song Contest	20
Events	51
Excelsior Hotel Baku	60
Explore	66

F

Face	197
Fashion	140
Female	40
Finestra	179
Finnegan's	197
Firuze	180
Flame Towers	152
Flying Carpet Shop	138
Folk Music	143
Food & Drink	12
Football	126
Fountain Square	80, 146
Funicular	55

G

Garmon	142
Georgia	125
Georgian House	180
Getting There	30, 52
Ghaval	142
Gobustan Mud Volcanoes	21
Golf	124
Grill, The	182
Gourmet Shop	180
Government House	72
Grand Hotel Europe	61
Gubernator Cafe	180
Gucci	140
Gymnastics	128
Gyms	116

H

Hamam	25, 119
Harry's Bar	197
Hazz Cafe	182
Heydar Aliyev International Airport	30
Heydar Aliyev Palace	92
Heydar Aliyev Park	97
Heydar Aliyev Sports and Exhibition Complex	128
Hiring a Car	57
History Museum	89
Hong Kong	182
Husein Javid Street	147
Huseyn Javid Park	97
Hyatt Regency Baku	61
Hydrocarbons	4, 16

Index

I

Icheri Sheher	74
Il Gusto	182
Il Mosaico	183
Ilham Aliyev	10
Imereti	183
Infiniti	198
Instruments	142
International Art Festival	136
International Mugham Centre	163
Internet	45
Islam	6, 14
Istiglaliyyat Street	147
Izmir	183

J

Jale Shopping Centre	152
Jasmine & Siam	183
Jazz	11, 163

K

Kanan Huseynov's Carpet Shop	138
Karaoke	160
Karavan Saray	184
Keshla Bazaar	150
Khagani Centre	153
Khagani Park	98
Khatai.	82
Khazar Golden Beach Hotel & Resort	65, 123
Konti Bar	198

L

La Strada	184
La Taverna	184
Landmark Health Club, The	120
Landmark Hotel Baku	61
Language	42
Lavangi	13
Letter Of Invitation	34
Live Music	162
Living Room	198
Lotus	185

M

Mado	185
Madonna	198
Maharajah	185
Maiden's Tower	78
Mangal BBQ	185
Marco Polo	186
Markets & Bazaars	130, 148
Marshall's	199
Marshrutkas	53
Martyrs' Alley	98
May 28th Bazaar	150
Media	48
Metkarting	199
Metro	54
Mexicana	186
Mineral Water	40
Miniature Book Museum	90
Ministry of Culture and Tourism	17
Modern Baku	16
Modern Times	9
Money	44
Mountain Biking	125
Mugham	5, 12
Mugham Club	186
Museum Of Independence	88
Museum of Modern Art	83, 86
Museums	66, 88
Music	20, 142
Music Land	143
Musical Comedy Theatre	93

N

Naghara	142
Nagorno Karabakh	113
Nakhchivan	16, 112
Narcotics	34
Nargiz Plaza	153
Nasimi Bazaar	150
National	15
Neftchilar Prospect	28
New Airport Bazaar	149
Newspapers	48
Nightlife	192
Nizami	147
Northern Azerbaijan	106

O

Old City	5, 11, 18, 74, 147
Old City Inn	61
Old Forester	200
Opening Hours	50
Opera	22
Opera & Ballet Theatre	22, 93, 164
Outdoor Amusements	97

P

Palmira Shopping Centre	152
Park Bulvar	16, 152
Park Bulvar Food Court	187
Park Hyatt Baku	62
Park Inn Hotel Azerbaijan	62
Parks	66, 96
Paul's	187
Penjere	187
Philharmonic Hall	163
Phoenix Bar	200
Pizza Inn	187
Places To Stay	58
Police	39
Population	16
Public Holidays	51

Q

Qiz Qalasi Gallery	86, 136

R

Radio	49
Radisson Blu Plaza Hotel	62
Ramada Baku	65
Ramada Hotel Health Club	123
Red Lion	200
Refresh Bar	200
Religion	14
Residency Permit	34
Restaurants	154, 174
Room Bar	201
Russian & Azeri Theatre	94

S

Sabun Nga Spa	121
Sahil Park	100
Saloon Bar	201
Scalini	188
Shakespeare's	201
Shamakhi	8
Shark Bar	201
Shashlik	75
Shawarma No 1	188
Shilla	188
Shipping	135, 138
Shirvanshah	8
Shirvanshah's Palace	18, 79
Shopping	130, 152
Sizing (Clothes)	134
Skiing	125
Sky Bar	202
Southern Azerbaijan	110
Souvenirs	143
Soviet Rule	9
Spas & Fitness	114
Spectator Sports	114, 126
Spice Inn	188
Sports	29, 114
Stranger's	202
Street Food	159

Sultan Inn	202
Sultan Inn Boutique Hotel	62
Summer	38
Sunset Cafe	189

T

Tatyana Agababayeva	136
Taxi	55
Taze Bey Hamam	116
Tea Houses	158
Telephone	45
Television	49
Tequila Junction	203
Teze Bazaar	150
The Azerbaijan State Museum Of Art	85
The Boulevard	27, 72, 146
The Brewery	193
The Britannia	194
The Caledonia	194
The Crescent Beach Hotel	123
The Grill	182
The Landmark Health Club	120
Theatre	164
Theatres	66, 92, 164
Time	46
Tipping	47
Top Bar	203
Tortuga Pirate Bar	203
Tours & Sightseeing	102
Train	54
Trattoria La Olivia	189
Traveller's Cafe	190
Turkish Airlines	32
Turkmenchay Treaty	8

U

U Dali	190
UNESCO World Heritage Site	68

V

Vegetarian Food	158
Venue Directory	166
Versace	132
Vertigo Bar	203
Vineyards	135
Virtu Art Gallery	136
Visa	33, 35
Visiting	30

W

Walking	56
Watersports	122
Western Azerbaijan	109
Wi-Fi	46
Wine City	135
Wines	156
Winter	38
Wrestling	128

Y

Yashil (Green) Bazaar	151
Yeni Gallery	136
Yusif Mirza's Studio	86

Z

Zakura Bar & Dining	190
Zeynalabdin Taghiyev	89
Zeytun	190
Zorge Park	100
Zoroastrianism	6

www.liveworkexplore.com

Explorer Products

Check out www.liveworkexplore.com

Live Work Explore Guides

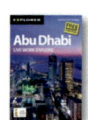

Also Available Amsterdam • Bahrain • Barcelona • Beijing • Berlin • Dublin
Geneva • Hong Kong • Kuala Lumpur • Kuwait • London • Los Angeles • New York
New Zealand • Oman • Paris • Shanghai • Singapore • Sydney • Tokyo • Vancouver

Mini Visitors' Guides

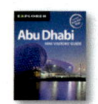

Also Available Amsterdam • Bahrain • Barcelona • Beijing • Dublin • London
Los Angeles • New York • New Zealand • Paris • Shanghai • Sharjah
Singapore • Sydney

Mini Maps

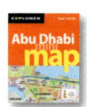

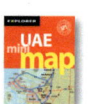

Also Available Amsterdam • Auckland • Bahrain • Barcelona • Beijing • Dublin
Hong Kong • Kuwait • London • Los Angeles • Muscat • New York • Paris
Ras Al Khaimah • Shanghai • Sharjah • Singapore • Sydney

Maps

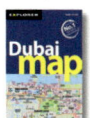

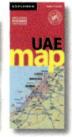

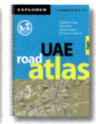

Photography Books

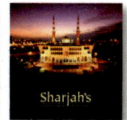

Practical & Lifestyle Products & Calendars

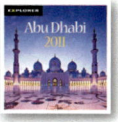

Activity Guides

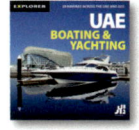

www.liveworkexplore.com

EXPLORER

Explorer Team
Check out www.liveworkexplore.com

Publishing
Founder & CEO Alistair MacKenzie
Associate Publisher Claire England

Editorial
Baku Mini Editor Tom Jordan
Editors Jo Iivonen, Matt Warnock,
Corporate Editor Charlie Scott
Web Editor Laura Coughlin
Production Coordinator Kathryn Calderon
Production Assistant Janette Tamayo
Sr Editorial Assistant Mimi Stankova
Editorial Assistants Amapola Castillo, Ingrid Cupido

Design & Photography
Creative Director Pete Maloney
Art Director Ieyad Charaf
Contract Publishing Manager Chris Goldstraw
Designer Michael Estrada
Junior Designer Didith Hapiz
Layout Manager Jayde Fernandes
Layout Designers Mansoor Ahmed, Shawn Zuzarte
Cartography Manager Zainudheen Madathil
Maps Administrator Ikumi Merola
Cartographers Dhanya Mellikunnummal, Noushad Madathil, Sunita Lakhiani
Image Editor Henry Hilos

IT & Digital Solutions
Digital Solutions Manager Derrick Pereira
Senior IT Administrator R. Ajay
Web Developer Anas Abdul Latheef

Sales & Marketing
Group Media Sales Manager Peter Saxby
Media Sales Area Managers Bryan Anes, Laura Zuffa, Pouneh Hafizi, Sabrina Ahmed, Yasin Alves
Corporate Solutions Account Manager Vibeke Nurgberg
Marketing Manager Lindsay Main
Sr Marketing Executive Stuart L. Cunningham
Sales & Marketing Assistant Shedan Ebona
Group Retail Sales Manager Ivan Rodrigues
Retail Sales Coordinator Michelle Mascarenhas
Senior Retail Sales Merchandisers Ahmed Mainodin, Firos Khan
Retail Sales Merchandisers Johny Mathew, Shan Kumar
Retail Sales Drivers Shabsir Madathil, Najumudeen K.I.
Warehouse Assistant Mohamed Haji

Finance & Administration
Administration Manager Fiona Hepher
Accountant Cherry Enriquez
Accounts Assistant Melody Beato, Sunil Suvarna
Reception & Admin Assistant Marie Joy Abarquez
Public Relations Officer Rafi Jamal
Office Assistant Shafeer Ahamed

Contact Us

▶ Register Online
Check out our new website for event listings, competitions and Dubai info, and submit your own restaurant reviews.
Log onto **www.explorerpublishing.com/dubai**

▶ Newsletter
Register online to receive Explorer's monthly newsletter and be first in line for our special offers and competitions.
Log onto **www.explorerpublishing.com**

▶ General Enquiries
We'd love to hear your thoughts and answer any questions you have about this book or any other Explorer product.
Contact us at **info@explorerpublishing.com**

▶ Careers
If you fancy yourself as an Explorer, send your CV (stating the position you're interested in) to **jobs@explorerpublishing.com**

▶ Contract Publishing
For enquiries about Explorer's Contract Publishing arm and design services contact **projects@explorerpublishing.com**

▶ Maps
For cartography enquiries, including orders and comments, contact **maps@explorerpublishing.com**

▶ Media and Corporate Sales
For bulk sales and customisation options, for this book or any Explorer product, contact **sales@explorerpublishing.com**

Notes